ESTATE PUBLICATIONS

HAMP!

GW00370675

NEW FOREST SHOW
SO 42 7QH
(7QH)

Street maps with index
Administrative Districts
Population Gazetteer
Road Map with index

Every effort has been made to verify the accuracy of information in this book but the publishers cannot accept responsibility for expense or loss caused by any error or omission. Information that will be of assistance to the user of the maps will be welcomed.

The representation of a road, track or footpath on the maps in this atlas is no evidence of the existence of a right of way.

Street plans prepared and published by ESTATE PUBLICATIONS, Bridewell House, TENTERDEN, KENT, and based upon the ORDNANCE SURVEY mapping with the permission of The Controller of H. M. Stationery Office.

The publishers acknowledge the co-operation of the local authorities of towns represented in this atlas.

COUNTY RED BOOK

HAMPSHIRE

contains street maps for each town centre

SUPER & LOCAL RED BOOKS

are street atlases with comprensive local coverage

BASINGSTOKE & ANDOVER

including: Alton, Heath End, Kingsclere, Oakley, Overton, Tadley, Whitchurch etc.

FAREHAM & GOSPORT

including: Lee-on-Solent, Portchester, Sarisbury, Stubbington, Titchfield, Warsash etc.

PORTSMOUTH

including: Clanfield, Denmead, Emsworth, Havant, Hayling Island, Petersfield, Southbourne, Southsea etc.

SOUTHAMPTON & EASTLEIGH

including: Bishopstoke, Cadham, Chandlers Ford, Hamble, Holbury, Hythe, Romsey, Wickham etc.

WINCHESTER

including: Kings Worthy, New Alresford, Twyford etc.

CONTENTS

HAMPSHIRE ADMINISTRATIVE DISTRICTS: pages 4—5

GAZETTEER INDEX TO ROAD MAP: pages 6—7
(with populations)

HAMPSHIRE ROAD MAP: pages 8—11
Scale: 4 miles to 1 inch

TOWN CENTRE STREET MAPS:

INDEX TO STREETS   pages 55—69

Scale of street plans: 4 inches to 1 mile (unless otherwise stated on map)

LEGEND TO STREET PLANS

One-way street	→	Post Office	●
Pedestrianized	▨	Public Convenience	Ⓒ
Car Park	Ⓟ	Place of worship	✛

The representation of a road, track or footpath on the maps in this atlas
is no evidence of the existence of a right of way

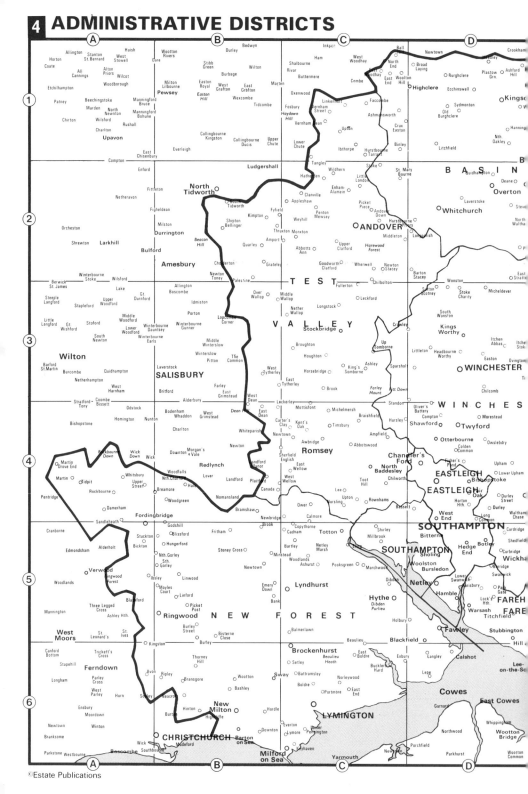

4 ADMINISTRATIVE DISTRICTS

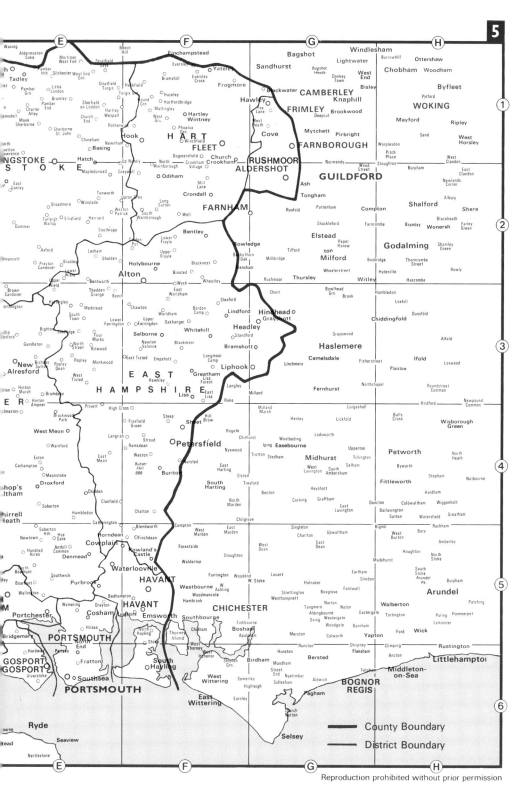

GAZETTEER INDEX TO ROAD MAP
with Populations

County of Hampshire population 1,541,547

Districts:

Basingstoke & Deane	144,790
East Hampshire	103,460
Eastleigh	105,990
Fareham	99,262
Gosport	75,061
Hart	80,921
Havant	119,697
New Forest	160,456
Portsmouth	174,697
Rushmoor	82,526
Southampton	196,864
Test Valley	101,428
Winchester	96,386

Abbotswood		10 D1
Abbotts Ann 1,316		8 B4
Abbots Barton 26		*
Aldershot 33,746		9 H3
Alton 16,356		9 F4
Alverstoke		11 F4
Ampfield 1,523		8 C6
Amport 1,093		8 B4
Andover. 35,064		8 C3
Andover Down		8 C3
Anthill Common		11 G2
Appleshaw 510		8 B3
Ashford Hill 1,160		8 D1
Ashley 56		8 C5
Ashmansworth 219		8 C2
Ashurst & Colbury 2,072		10 C2
Avon		10 A4
Awbridge 685		10 C1
Axford		9 E4
Badger Farm 2,415		*
Ball Hill		8 C1
Balmerlawn		10 C3
Bank		10 C3
Bartley		10 C2
Barton on Sea		10 B4
Barton Stacey 741		8 C4
Bashley		10 B4
Basingstoke 73,662		9 E3
Bassett		10 D1
Battramsley		10 C4
Baughurst 2,448		9 E2
Beaulieu 726		10 D3
Beauworth 88		*
Bedhampton		11 G3
Beech		9 F4
Bentley 873		9 G4
Bentworth 550		9 F4
Bickton		10 A2
Bighton 336		9 E5
Binley		8 C2
Binsted 1,706		9 G4
Bishops Sutton 414		9 E5
Bishopstoke		11 E1
Bishop's Waltham 6,037		11 F1
Bisterne Close		10 B3
Bitterne		11 E2
Blackfield		10 D3
Blackmoor		9 G5
Blacknest		9 G4
Blackwater		9 H2
Blashford		10 A3
Blendworth		11 H2
Blissford		10 B2
Boarhunt 465		11 F2
Boldre 1,969		10 C4
Bordon Camp		9 G5
Bossington 53		*
Botley 4,969		11 E2
Bradley 116		9 F4
Braishfield 633		8 C6
Bramdean 500		9 E6
Bramley 2,278		9 F2
Bramshaw 649		10 C1
Bramshill 190		9 G2
Bramshott and Liphook 7,351		9 H5
Bransgore 4,630		10 B4
Breamore 345		10 A1
Bridgemary		11 F3
Broad Laying		8 C1
Broadmere		9 E3
Brockenhurst 3,322		10 C3
Brockwood Park		9 E6
Brook (Horsebridge)		8 B6

Broughton 1,022		8 B5
Brown Candover		9 E4
Buckholt 15		*
Bucklers Hard		10 D3
Bullington 104		*
Burghclere 1,193		8 D2
Buriton 716		11 H1
Burley 1,438		10 B3
Burley St		10 B3
Burridge		11 F2
Bursledon 5,629		11 E2
Cadnam		10 C2
Calmore		10 C2
Calshot		11 E3
Canada		10 C1
Candovers 207		*
Carter's Clay		8 B6
Catherington		11 G2
Chalton		11 H2
Charlton 2,082		*
Chandler's Ford		10 D1
Charter Alley		9 E2
Chawton 359		9 F4
Cheriton 603		9 E6
Chidden		11 G1
Chilbolton 1,018		8 C4
Chilcomb 95		8 D6
Chilworth 1,932		10 D1
Chineham 5,856		9 F2
Church Crookham		9 G3
Church End		9 F2
Clanfield 3,924		11 G1
Clanville		8 B3
Cliddesden 457		*
Colden Common 3,065		11 E1
Colemore and Priors Dean 129		*
Compton & Shawford 1,582		8 D6
Copythorne 2,631		10 C2
Corhampton & Meonstoke 602		11 F1
Cosham		11 G3
Cove		9 H2
Cowplain 9,361		11 G2
Crawley 392		8 C5
Crondall 4,490		9 G3
Crookham Village 1,300		9 G3
Crux Easton		8 C2
Curbridge 1,211		11 F2
Curdridge		11 F2
Damerham 536		10 A1
Dean		11 F1
Deane 80		8 D3
Denmead 5,626		11 G2
Denny Lodge 357		*
Dibden (with Hythe) 19,293		10 D2
Dogmersfield 323		9 G3
Downton		10 C4
Drayton		11 G3
Droxford 663		11 G1
Dummer 422		9 E3
Durley 830		11 F1
Durley St		11 F1
E. Boldre 787		10 D3
E. Dean 197		8 A6
E. End (Highclere)		8 C2
E. End (Lymington)		10 D4
E. Hayling (with West) 16,016		11 H3
Eastleigh 60,699		11 E1
E. Liss		9 G6
E. Meon 1,177		11 G1
E. Oakley		9 E3
Easton		8 D5
E. Stratton		9 E4
E. Tisted 181		9 F5
E. Tytherley 200		8 B5
E. Wellow 3,227		10 C1
E. Woodhay 2,598		8 C1
E. Worldham		9 G4
Ecchinswell and Symondton 1,175		8 D2
Eling (with Totton) 26,176		10 D2
Ellingham, Harbridge & Ibsley 1,132		10 A2
Ellisfield 273		9 F3
Emery Down		10 C2
Empshott		9 G5
Emsworth 9,692		11 H3
Enham Alamein		8 B3
Eversley 1,300		9 G1
Eversley Cross		9 G2

Everton		10 C4
Exbury and Lepe 156		10 D3
Exton 164		11 G1
Faccombe 103		8 C2
Fair Oak & Horton Heath 8,016		11 E1
Fareham 32,703		11 F3
Farleigh Wallop 92		9 E3
Farnborough 48,780		9 H2
Farringdon (Uppr & Lwr) 538		9 F5
Fawley. 13,732		11 E3
Finchdean		11 H2
Fishers Pond		11 E1
Fleet 21,132		9 G2
Fordingbridge 5,792		10 A2
Four Marks 2,814		9 F5
Fox La		9 H2
Fratton		11 G3
Frenchmoor 33		*
Fritham		10 B2
Frogmore		9 H2
Froxfield Grn 821		9 F6
Fullerton		8 B4
Funtley		11 F2
Fyfield 440		8 B3
Godshill		10 B2
Golden Pot		9 F4
Goodworth Clatford 695		8 B4
Gosport 67,802		11 F3
Grateley 579		8 A4
Grayshott 2,113		9 H5
Greatham 786		9 G5
Greywell 225		9 F3
Gundleton		9 E5
Hale 535		10 B1
Hamble 3,229		11 E3
Hambledon 876		11 G2
Hannington 319		9 E2
Hardway		11 F3
Hartfordbridge		9 G2
Hartley Wespall 152		9 F2
Hartley Wintney 5,011		9 G2
Hatch		9 F3
Hatherden		8 B3
Hattingley		9 F4
Havant 73,271		11 H2
Hawkley 447		9 G5
Hawley 5,365		9 H2
Hazeley		9 G2
Headbourne Worthy 443		8 D5
Headley (Heath End)		8 D1
Headley (Liphook) 5,607		9 H5
Heath End		9 E1
Heckfield 298		9 F2
Hedge End 13,499		11 E2
Herriard 223		9 F3
Highclere 1,403		8 C2
High Cross		9 F6
Hill Head 7,843		11 F3
Hilsea		11 G3
Hinton		10 B4
Hinton Ampner		9 E6
Hinton Marsh		9 E6
Hoe Gate		11 G2
Holbury		10 D3
Holyourne		9 G4
Hook 6,003		9 F2
Hordle 4,875		10 C4
Horndean 11,985		11 H2
Horsebridge		8 B5
Horton Hth. & Fair Oak 8,016		11 E1
Houghton 391		8 B5
Hound Grn 6,775		9 G2
Hundred Acres		11 F2
Hungerford		10 B2
Hursley 792		8 C6
Hurstbourne Priors 337		8 C3
Hurstbourne Tarrant 700		8 C2
Hyde 920		*
Hythe (with Dibden) 19,293		10 D3
Ibthorpe		8 C2
Ibworth		9 E2
Itchen Abbas		8 D5
Itchen Stoke and Ovington 243		9 E5
Itchen Valley 1,222		*
Kent's Oak		8 B6

Population figures are based upon the 1991 census and relate to the local authority area or parish as constituted at that date   Boundaries of the districts are shown on pages 4-5. Places with no population figure form part of a larger local authority area or parish.

Population figures in bold type.

*Place not included on map due to limitation of space.

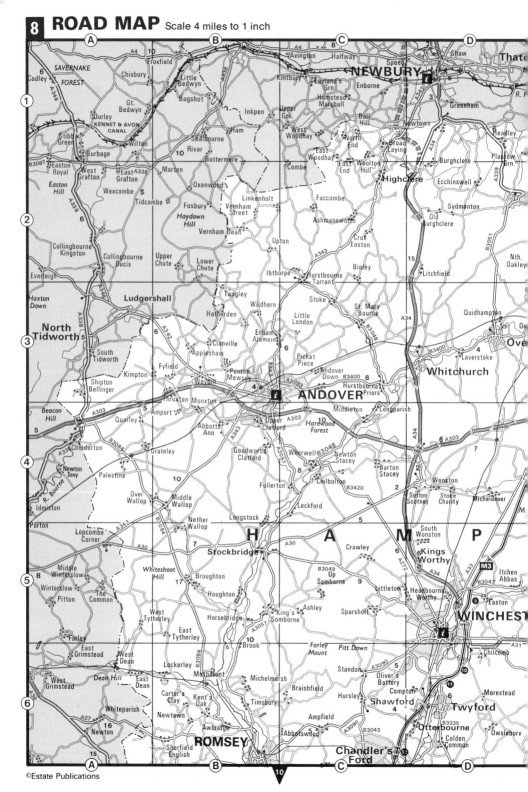

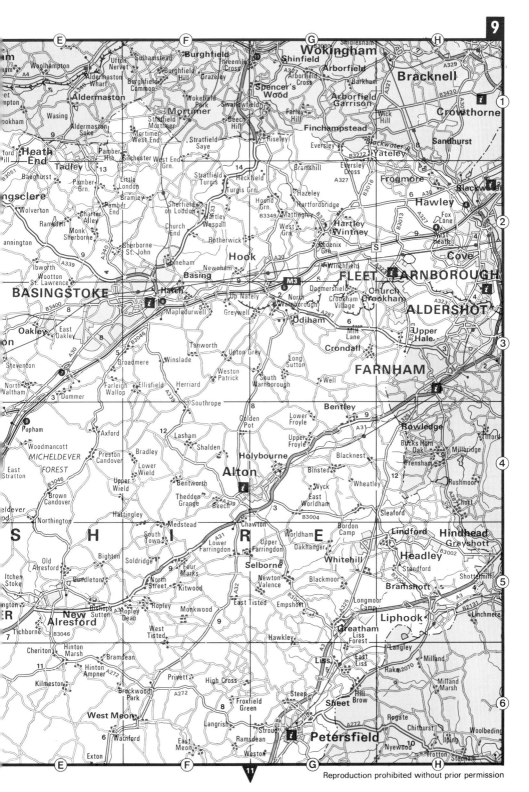

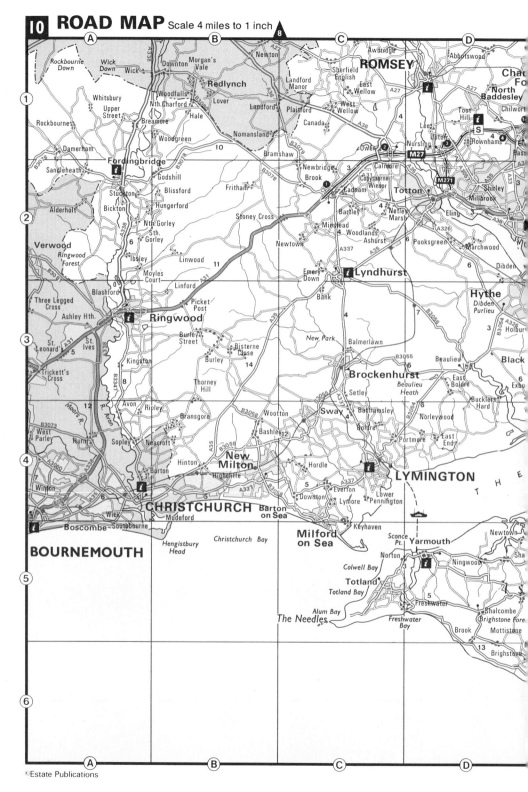

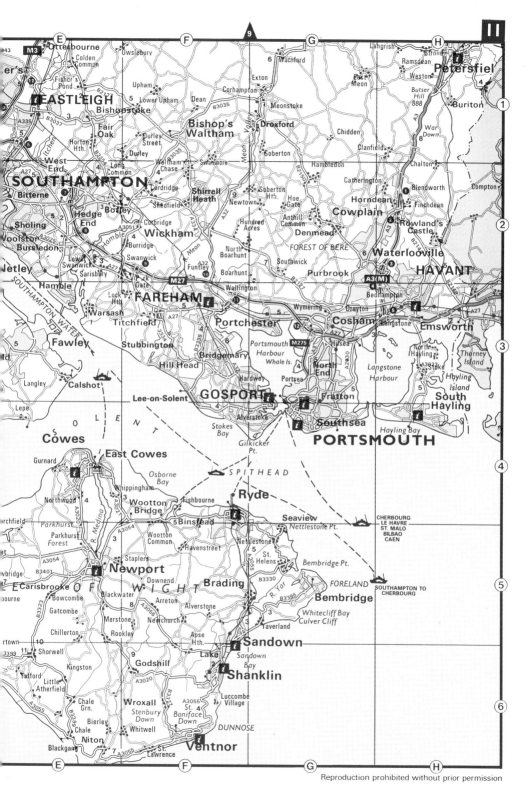

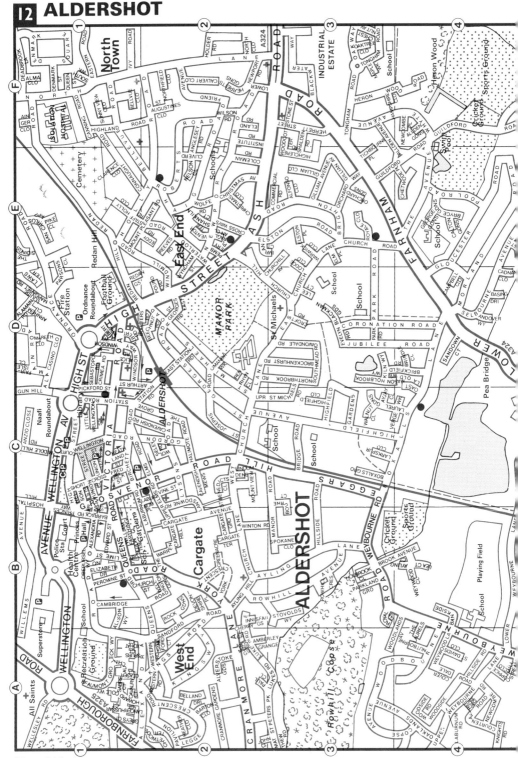

ALTON

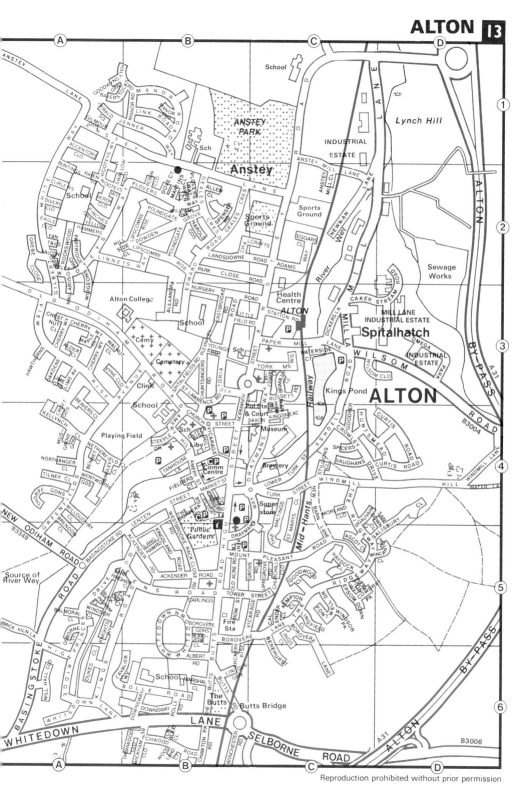

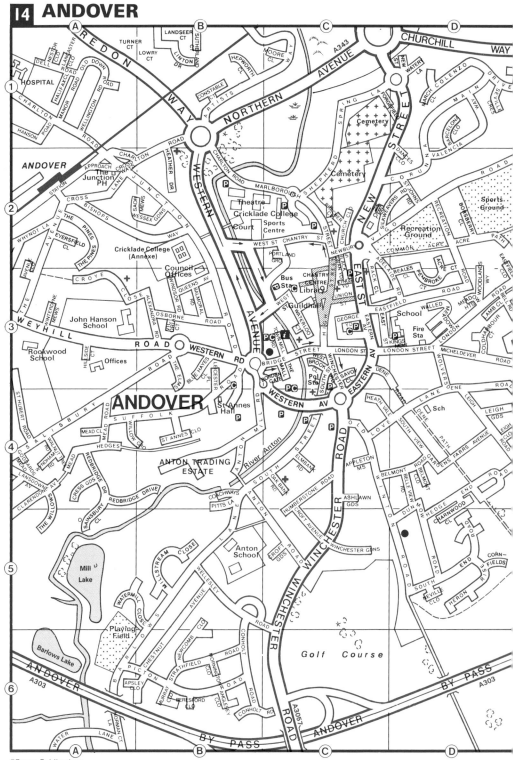

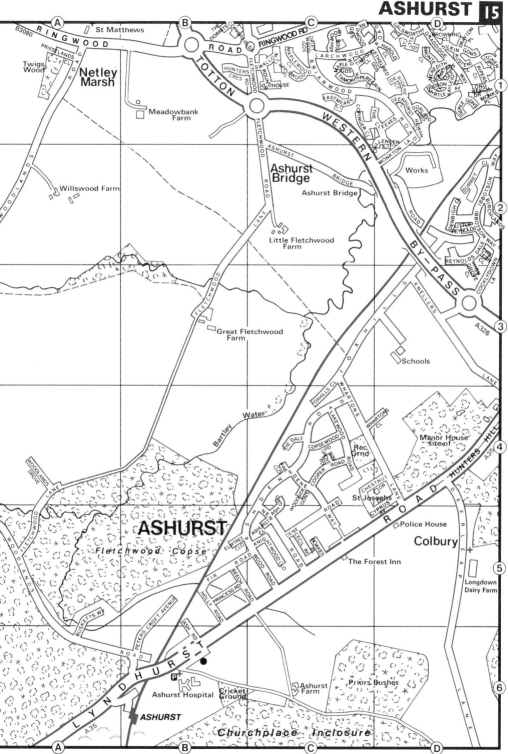

ASHURST 15

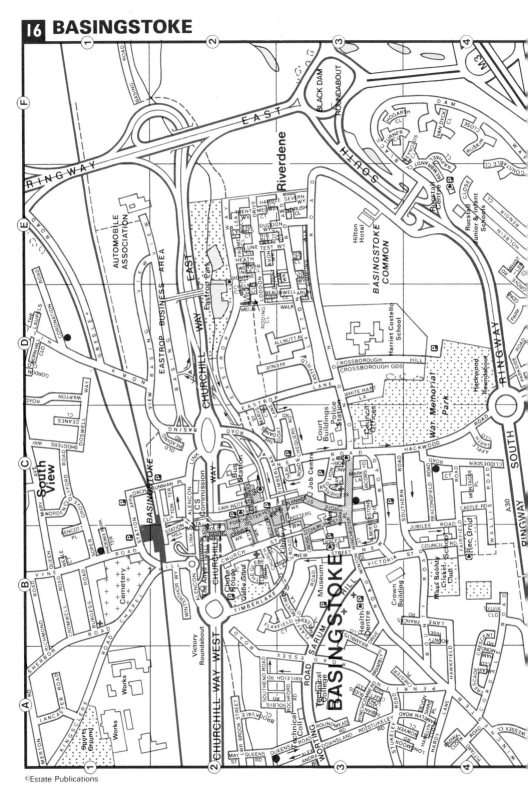

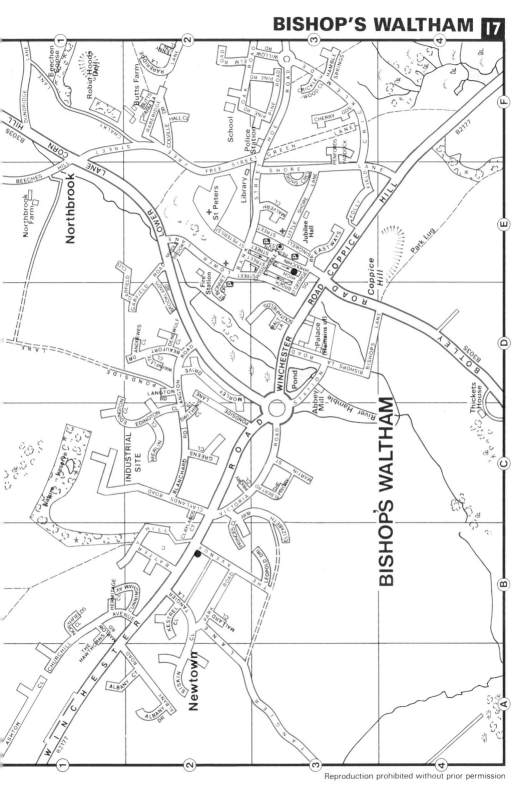

BISHOP'S WALTHAM

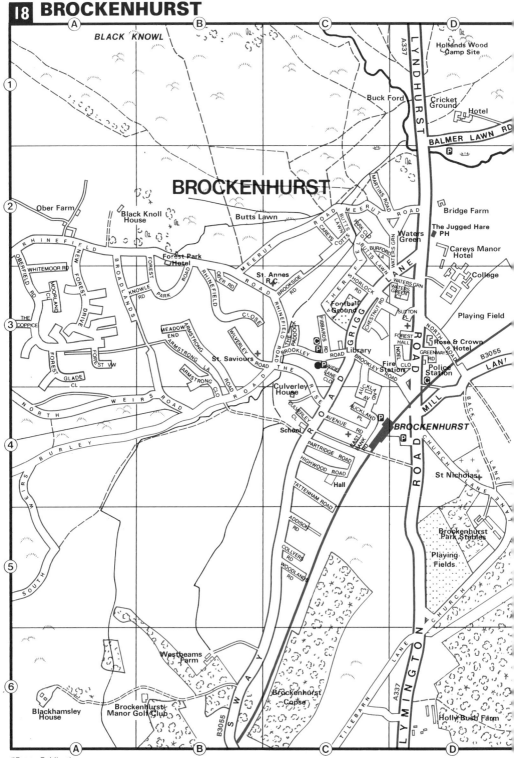

BROCKENHURST

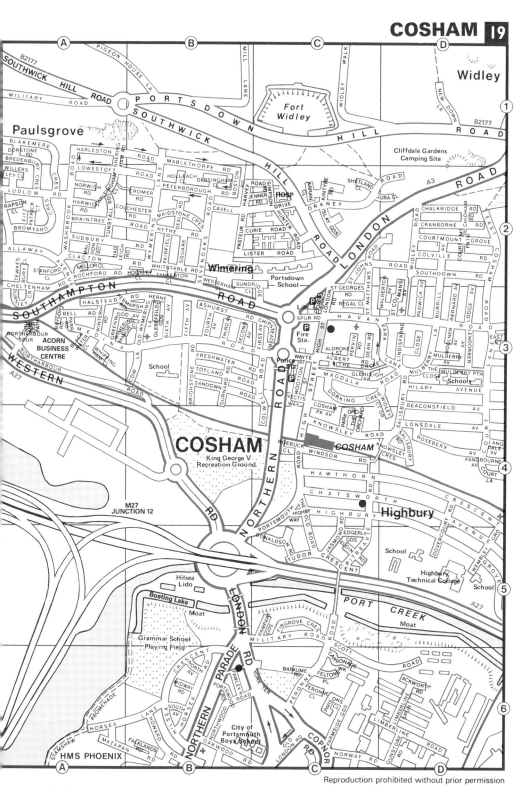

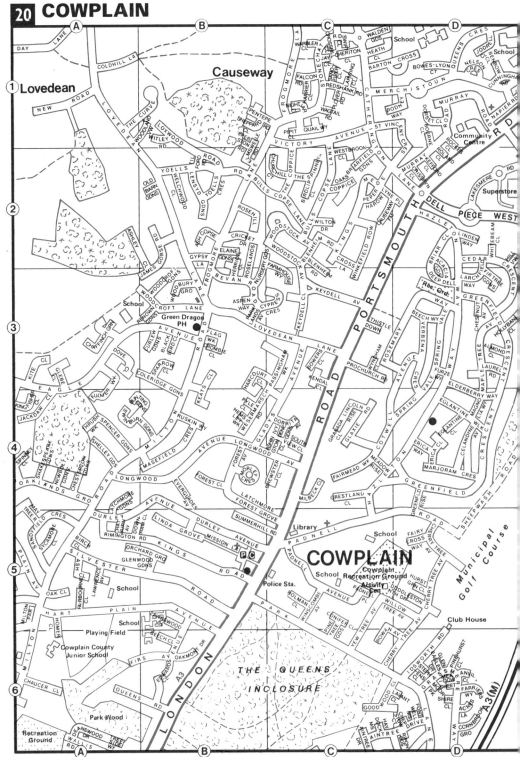

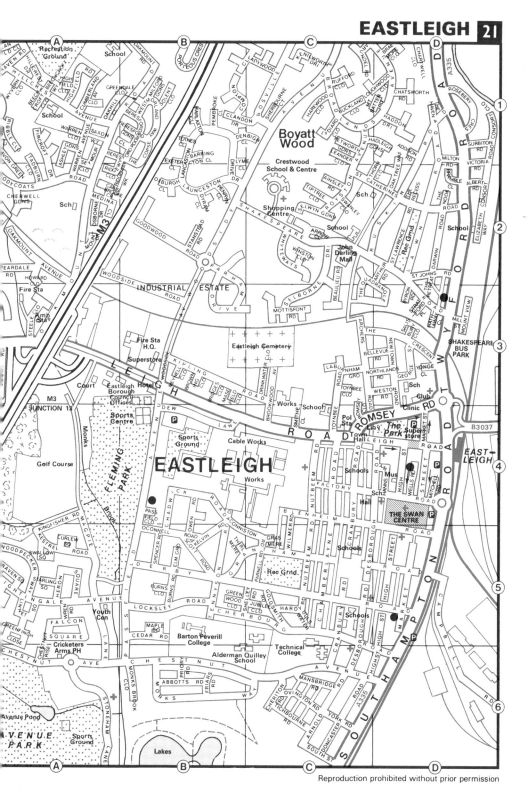

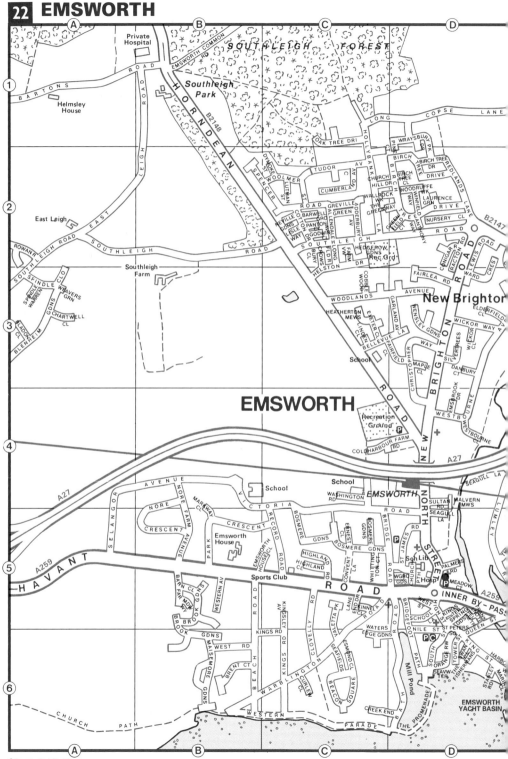

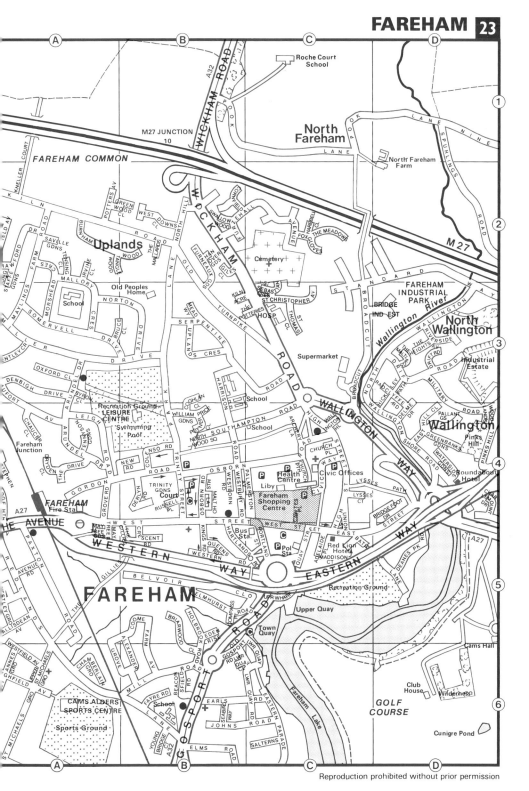

24 FARNBOROUGH

©Estate Publications

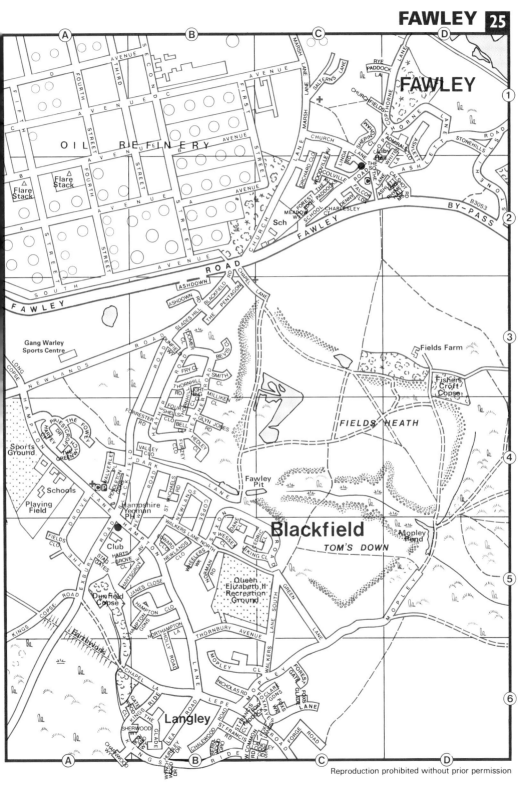

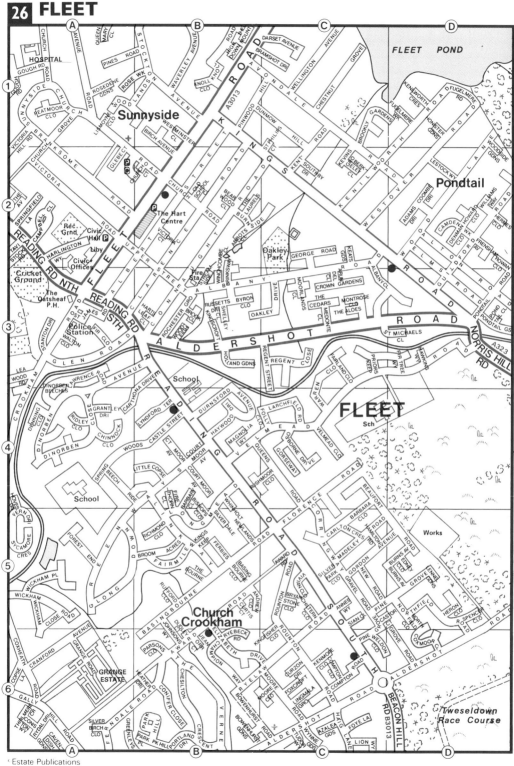

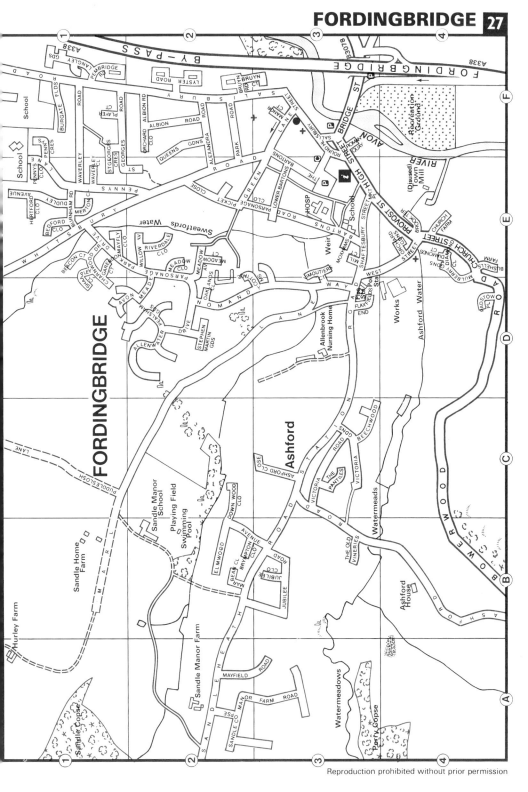

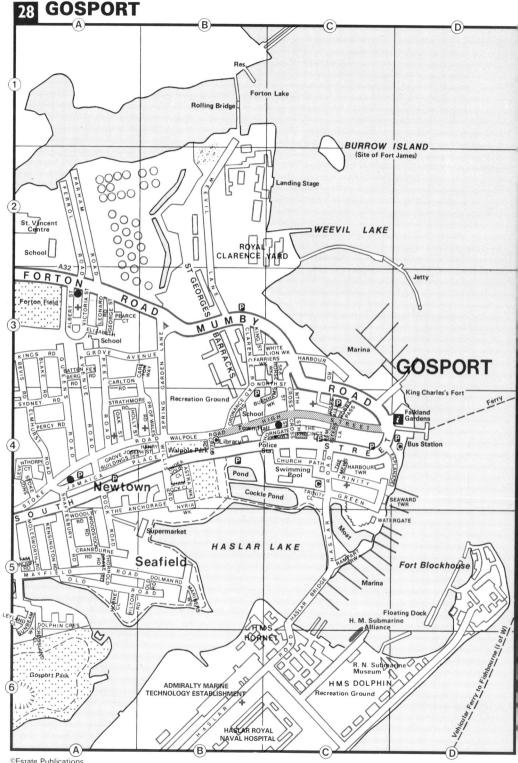

Res.

Forton Lake

Rolling Bridge

BURROW ISLAND
(Site of Fort James)

Landing Stage

St. Vincent Centre

School

WEEVIL LAKE

ROYAL CLARENCE YARD

Jetty

A32

FORTON ROAD

Forton Field

MUMBY

BARRACKS

Marina

GOSPORT

King Charles's Fort

Ferry

Recreation Ground

Falkland Gardens

School

Town Hall

Bus Station

Library

Police Sta.

Walpole Park

Swimming Pool

HARBOUR TWR

Newtown

Pond

TRINITY

SEAWARD TWR

Cockle Pond

TRINITY CL

GREEN

WATERGATE

Supermarket

HASLAR LAKE

Fort Blockhouse

Seafield

Moat

Marina

Floating Dock

H. M. Submarine
Alliance

Gosport Park

HMS HORNET

R. N. Submarine Museum

HMS DOLPHIN
Recreation Ground

ADMIRALTY MARINE
TECHNOLOGY ESTABLISHMENT

HASLAR ROYAL
NAVAL HOSPITAL

Vehicular Ferry to Fishbourne (I of W)

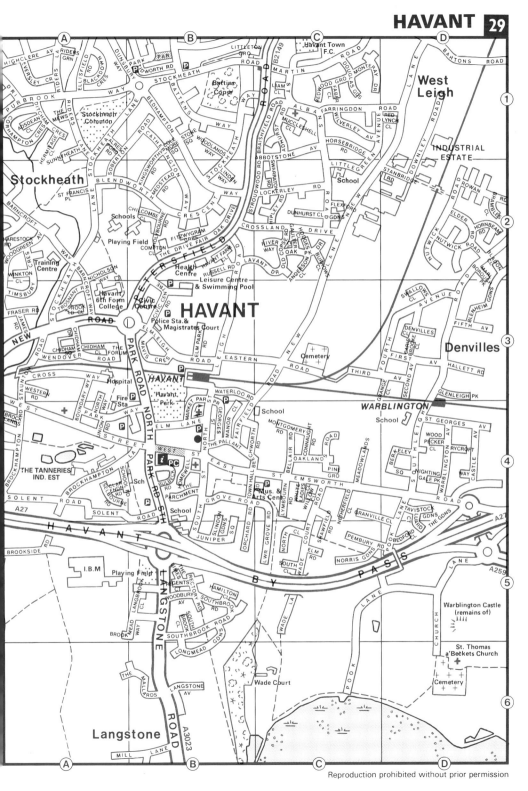

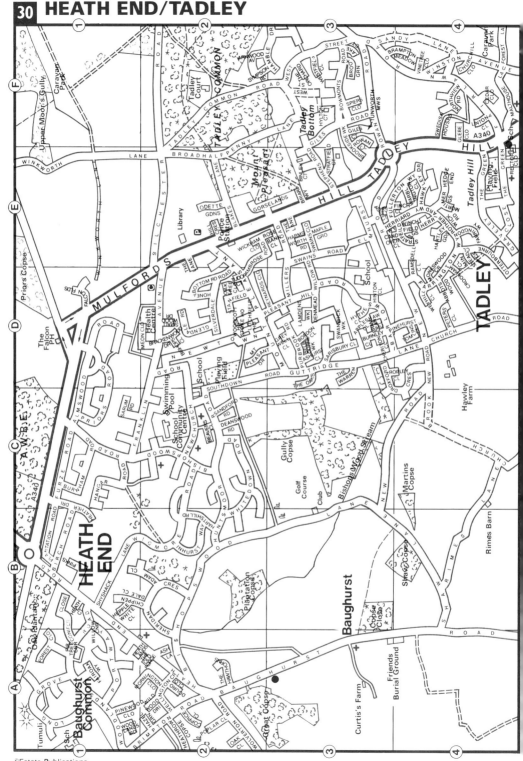

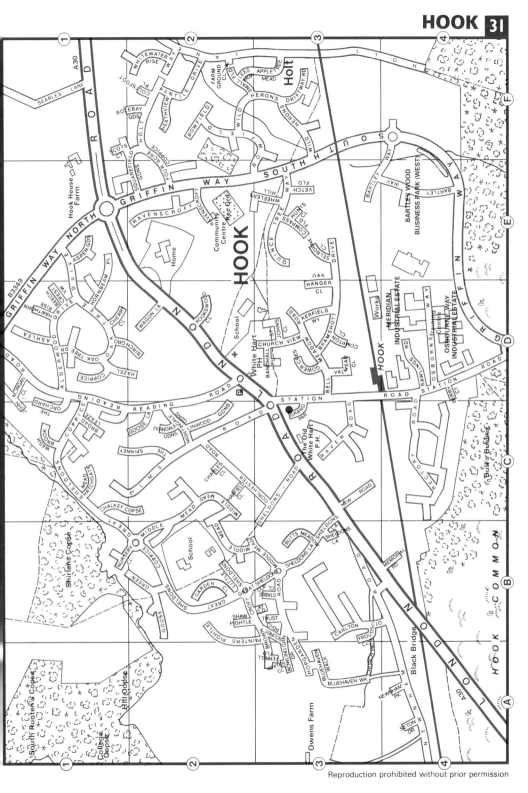

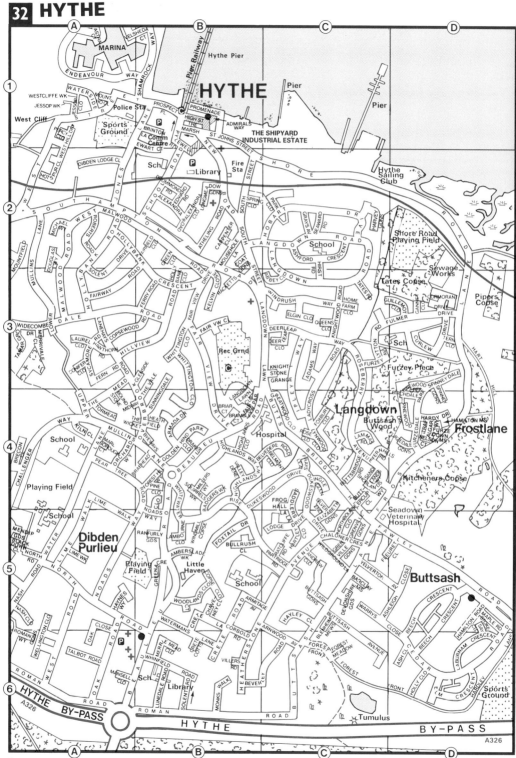

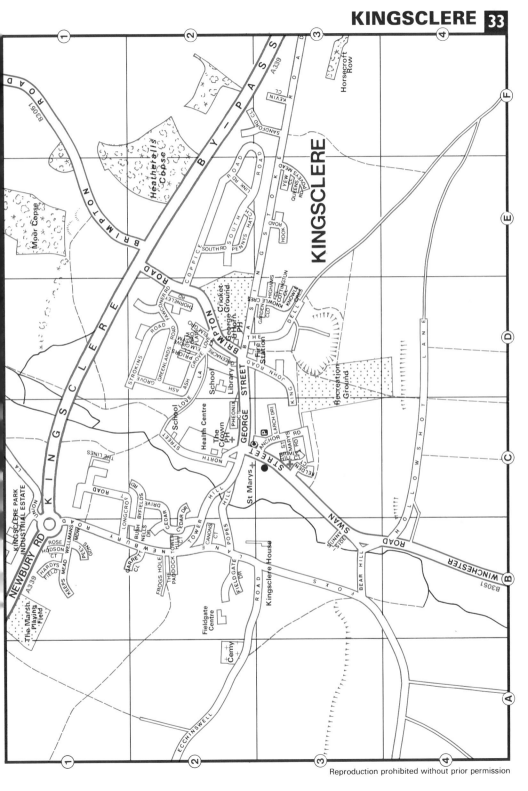

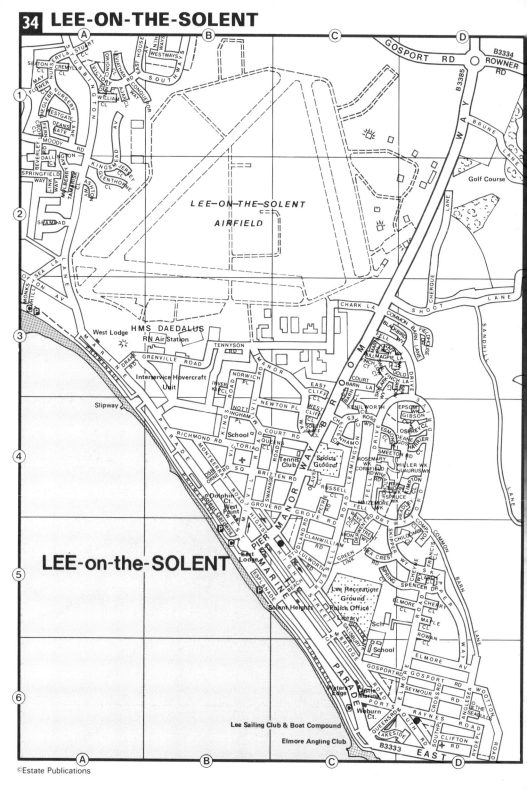

LEE-on-the-SOLENT

LEE-ON-THE-SOLENT AIRFIELD

HMS DAEDALUS
RN Air Station

Interservice Hovercraft Unit

Golf Course

GOSPORT RD

ROWNER RD

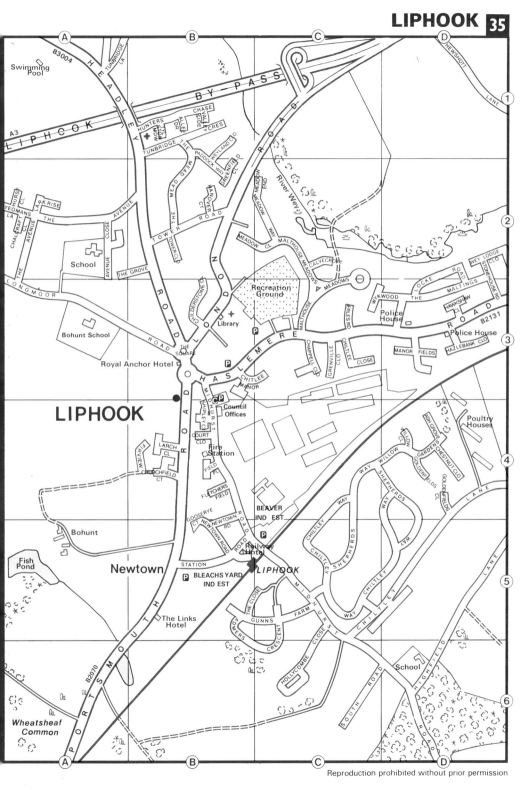

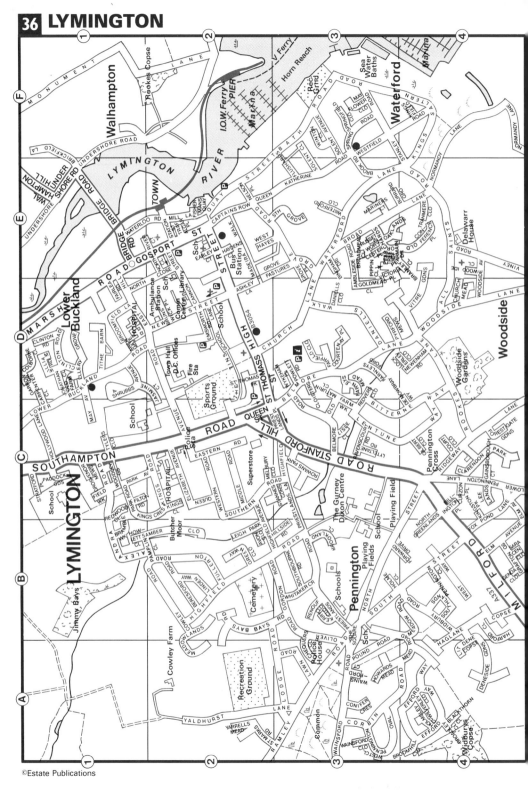

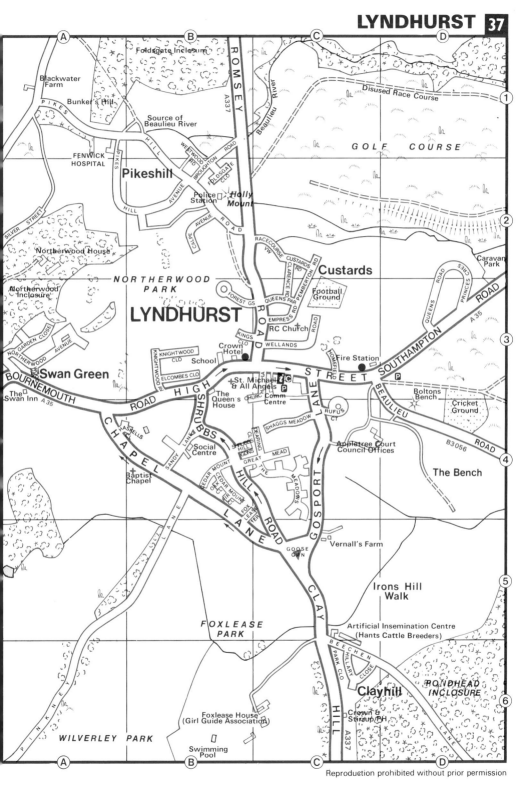

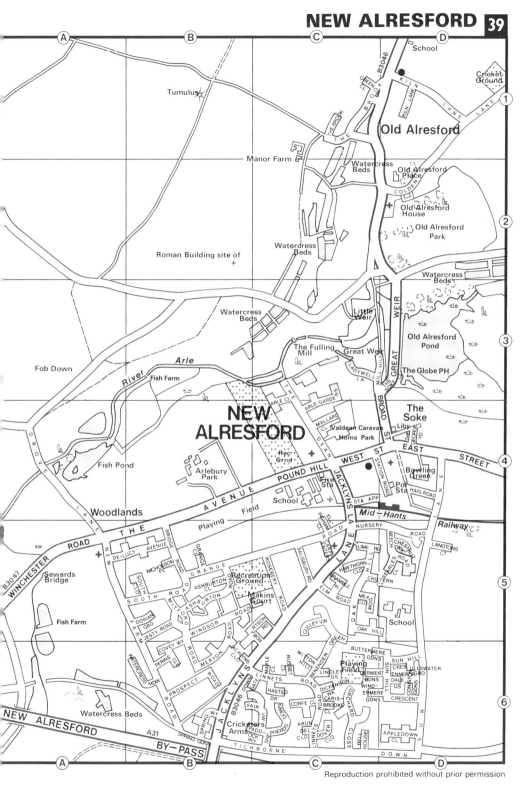

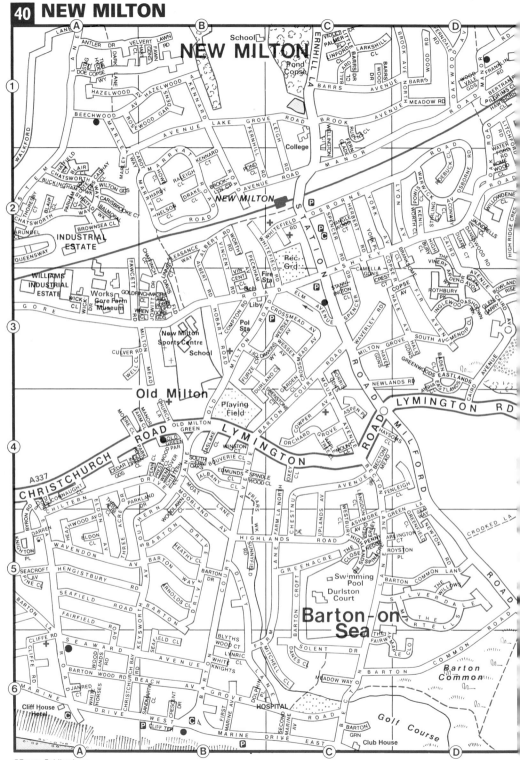

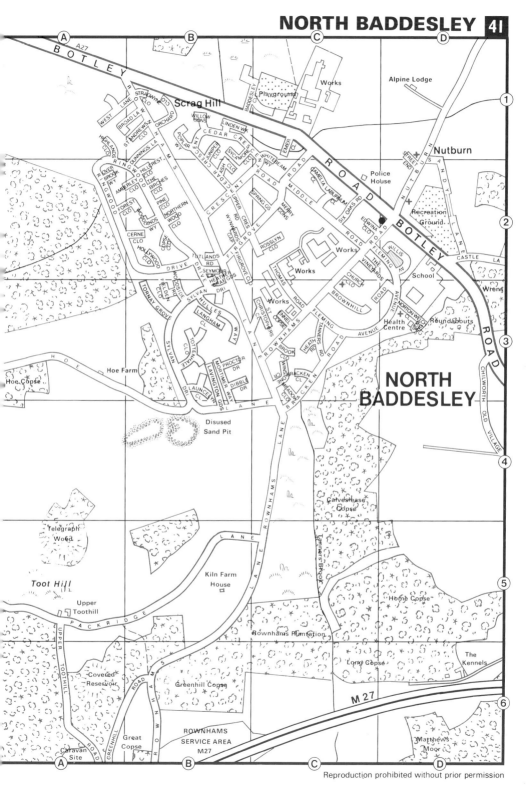

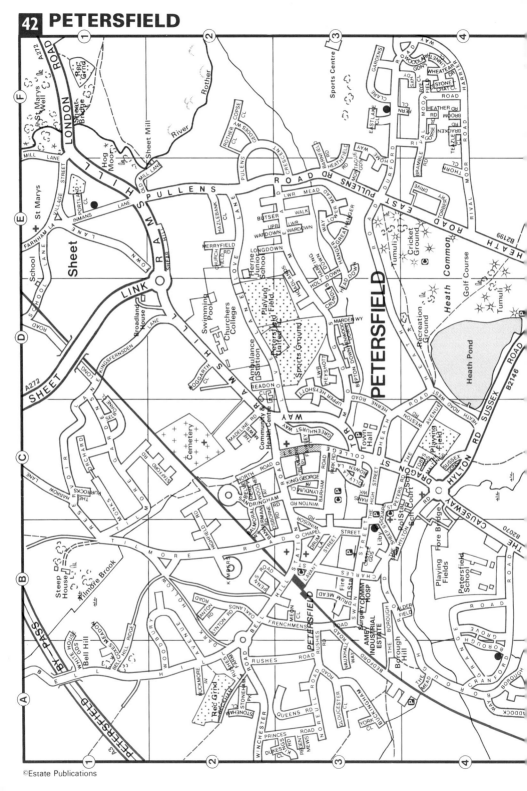

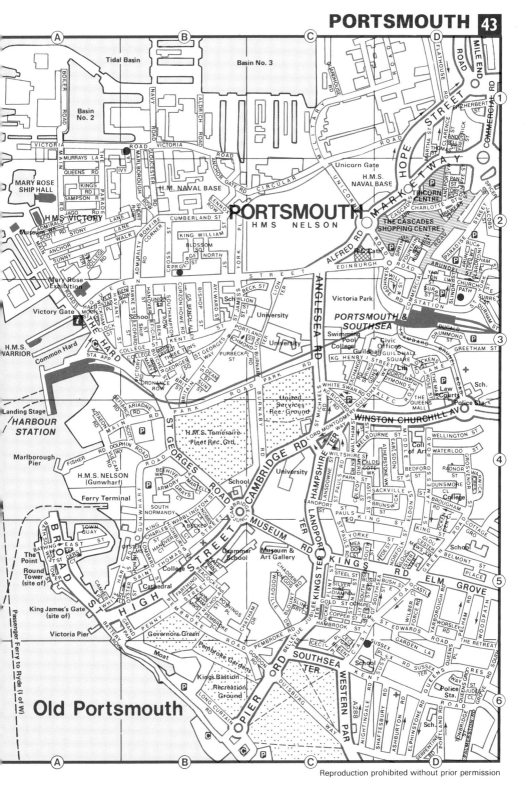

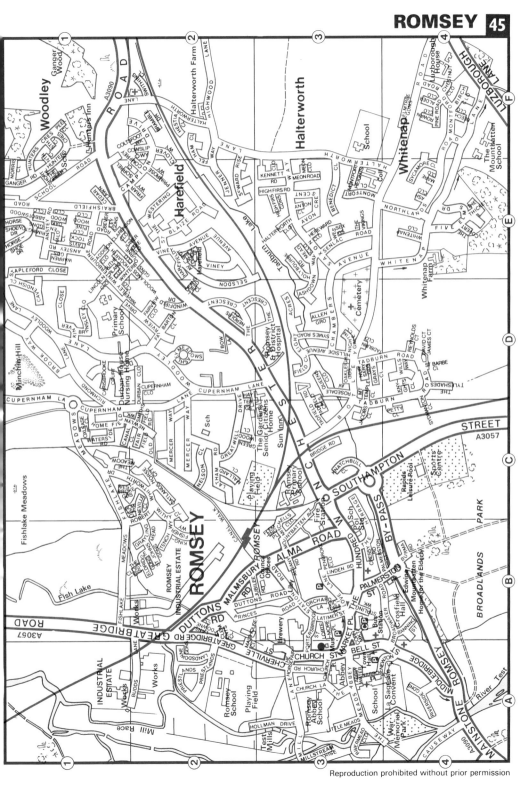

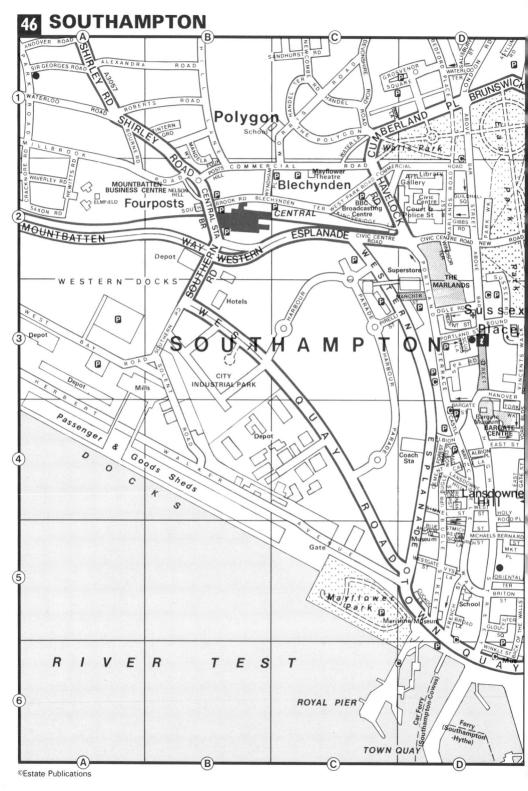

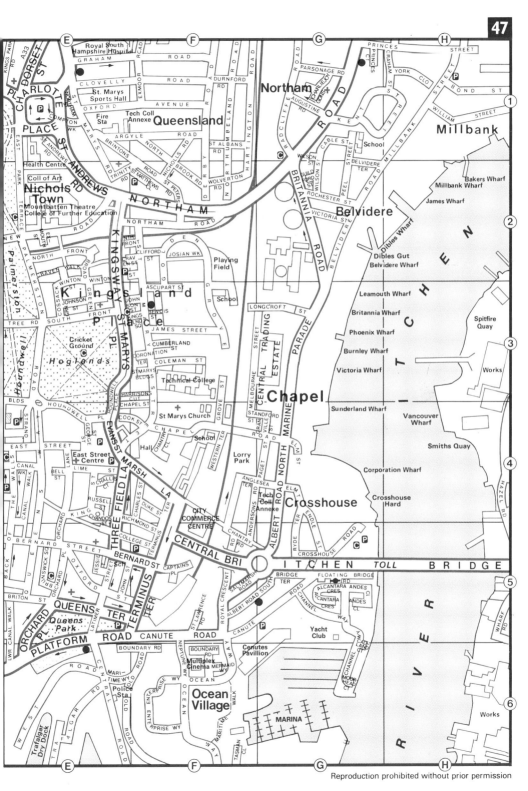

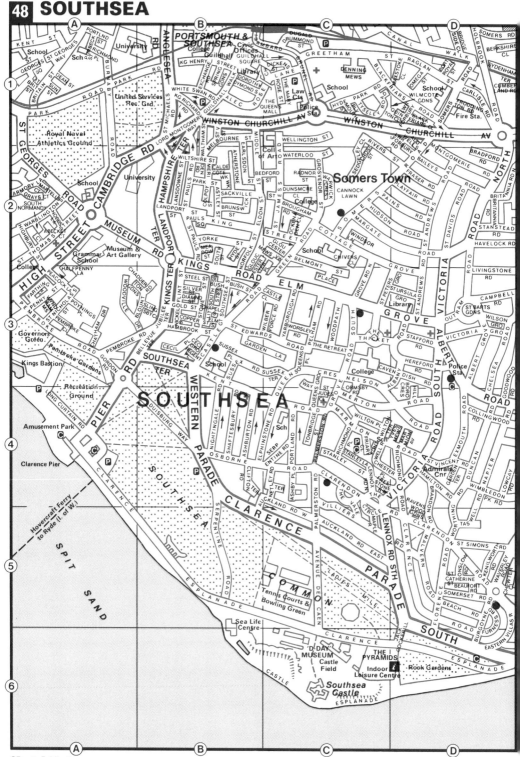

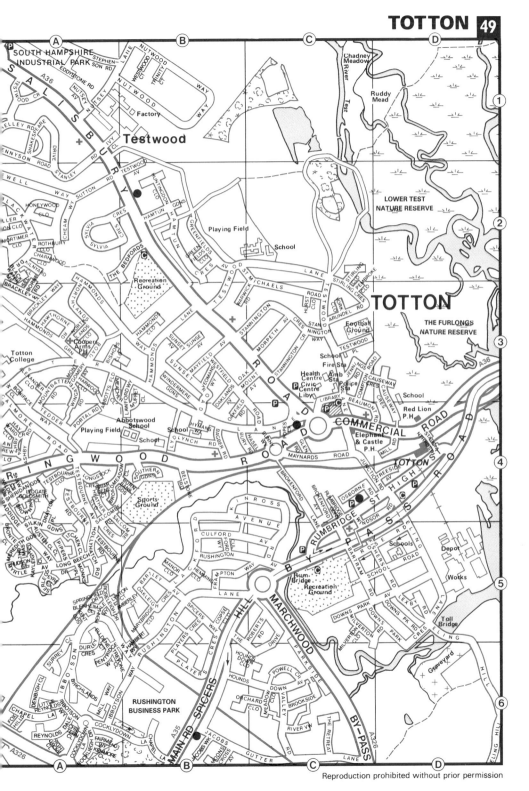

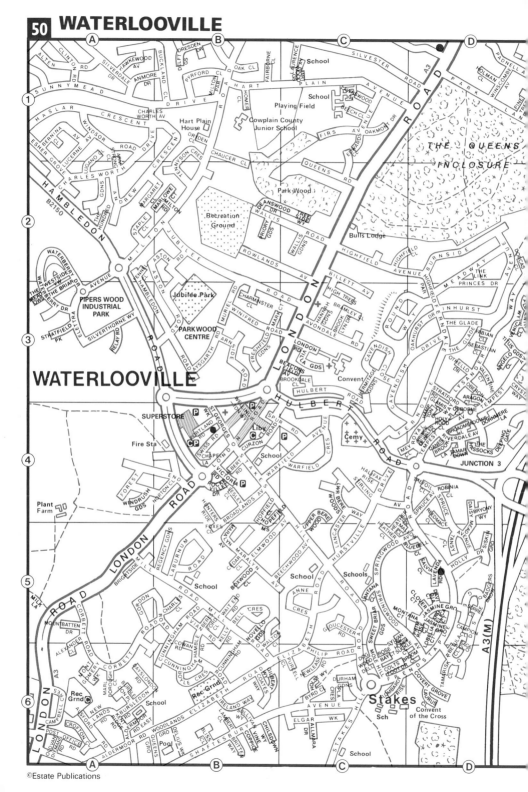

WATERLOOVILLE

THE QUEENS INCLOSURE

PIPERS WOOD INDUSTRIAL PARK

PARKWOOD CENTRE

SUPERSTORE

Recreation Ground

Jubilee Park

Park Wood

Cowplain County Junior School

Hart Plain House

Playing Field

School

School

Bulls Lodge

Convent

Cemy

JUNCTION 3

Plant Farm

Stakes

Convent of the Cross

Rec Grnd

Rec Grnd

School

School

School

School

School

Schools

Fire Sta

Liby

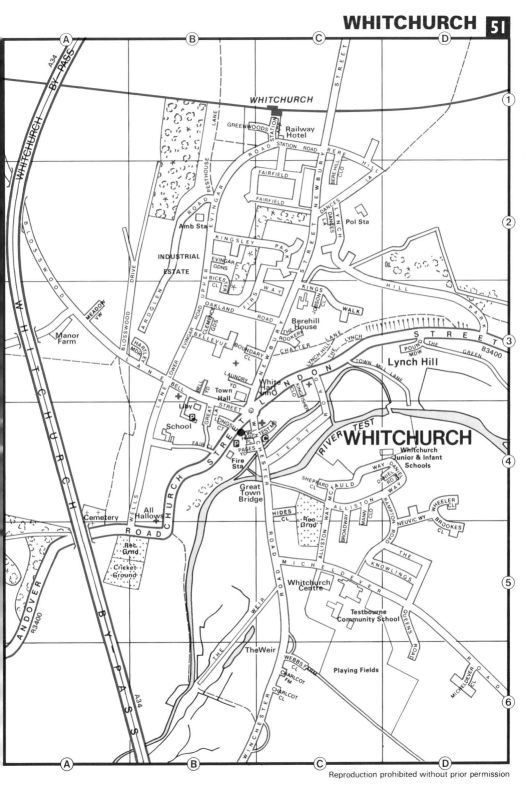

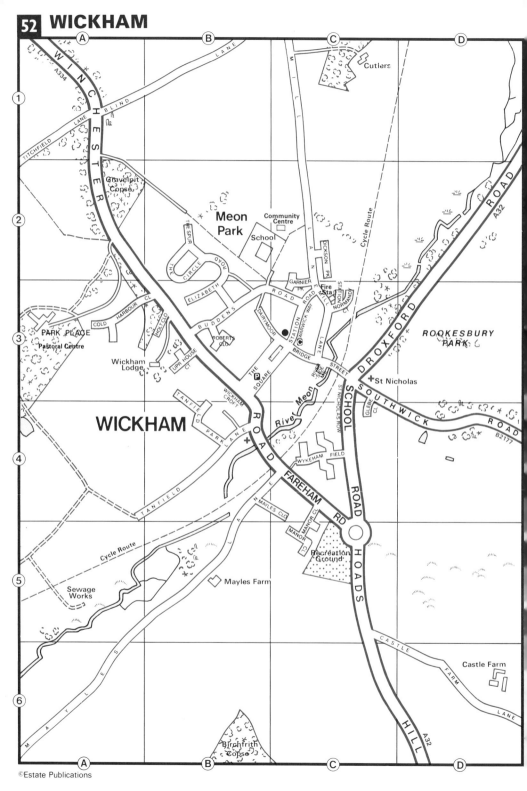

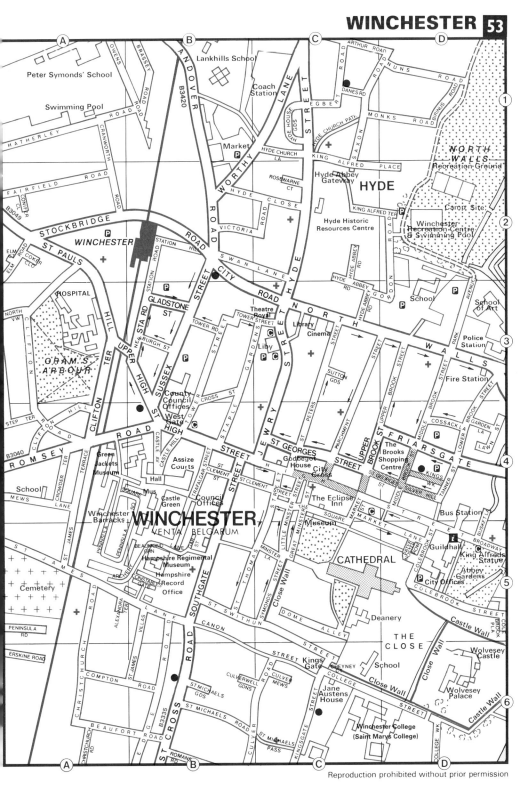

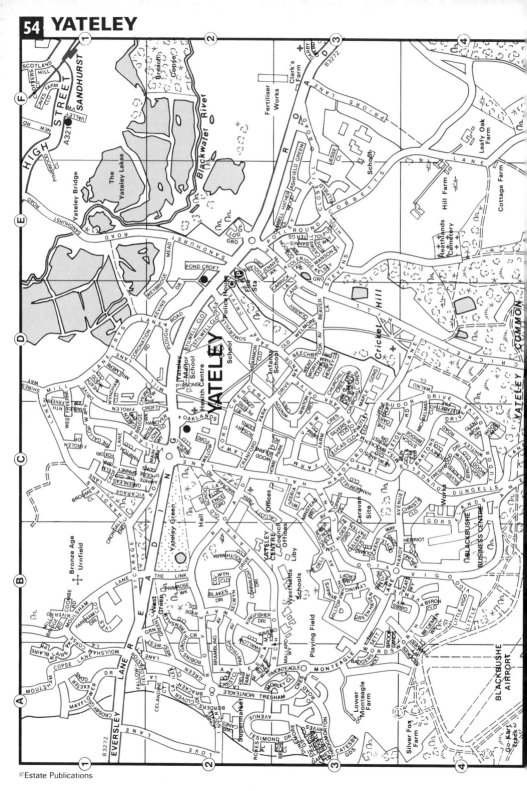

A - Z INDEX TO STREETS

Mill La	13 C1	Artists Way	14 B1	Pembroke Ct	14 D3
Morland Clo	13 C4	Avenue Clo	14 A3	Picton Rd	14 A6
Mount Pleasant Rd	13 B5	Balmoral Rd	14 B3	Pitts La	14 B4
Musgrove Gdns	13 A4	Barcelona Clo	14 D1	Portland Gro	14 C2
*Nether St,		Barlows La	14 A6	Queens Av	14 B3
Normandy St	13 C3	Beales Clo	14 D3	Rack Clo	14 C3
Netherfield Clo	13 A4	Bell Rd	14 D3	Recreation Rd	14 D2
New Barn La	13 C4	Belle Vue Rd	14 D4	Redbridge Dri	14 A4
New Odiham Rd	13 A4	Belmont Clo	14 D4	Redon Way	14 A1
Newman La	13 C2	Belmont Rd	14 C4	Sainsbury Clo	14 A5
Normandy St	13 B4	Beresford Clo	14 B6	St Annes Clo	14 B4
Northanger Clo	13 A4	Bishops Way	14 A2	St Hubert Rd	14 A4
Nursery Rd	13 B3	Black Swan Yd	14 C2	St Johns Rd	14 D2
Oakdene	13 A3	Blue Hayes Clo	14 B3	Salisbury Rd	14 A4
Old Acre Rd	13 B5	Borden Gate	14 C3	Saor Mews	14 A2
Old Odiham Rd	13 A3	Borsberry Clo	14 D2	Savoy Clo	14 C3
Oliver Rise	13 B4	Bracher Clo	14 C2	Seville Cres	14 D1
Orchard La	13 C3	Bridge St	14 C3	Shepherd Spring La	14 C2
Osborne Clo	13 A5	Chantry St	14 C2	Silkweavers Rd	14 C2
Paper Mill La	13 C3	Chantry Way	14 C3	South End Rd	14 D5
Park Close Rd	13 B2	Charlton Rd	14 A1	South St	14 B4
Partridge Grn	13 A2	Charnwood Clo	14 D5	South Vw Gdns	14 D4
Plevna Pl	13 B3	Chestnut Av	14 B6	Station App	14 A2
Plovers Way	13 B2	Church Clo	14 C2	Strathfield Rd	14 B6
Plumpton Way	13 C5	Churchill Way	14 D1	Suffolk Rd	14 A4
Poundgate	13 B2	Clarendon Av	14 A4	Sutherland Ct	14 B1
Princes Dri	13 A5	Coachways	14 B4	The Avenue	14 A3
Queens Rd	13 B5	Colenzo Dri	14 D1	The Crossways	14 A2
Rack Close Rd	13 B5	Common Acre	14 D2	The Elms	14 B3
Raven Sq	13 A2	Conholt Rd	14 B6	The Mall	14 C3
Robin Clo	13 B2	Constable Ct	14 B1	The Pines	14 A2
Rookswood	13 A2	Cornfields	14 D5	The Willows	14 A4
Russett Rd	13 C3	Corunna Main	14 D2	Town Mill Rd	14 C3
St Lawrence Rd	13 B3	Cress Gdns	14 A4	Turner Ct	14 A1
St Marys Clo	13 C5	Croft Av	14 C5	Union St	14 C3
Salisbury Rd	13 C5	Cross La	14 A2	Valencia Way	14 D2
Sandown Clo	13 D4	Croye Clo	14 A3	Vigo Rd	14 C2
Sandringham Clo	13 A5	Dances Clo	14 D2	Walnut Tree Rd	14 A4
Saxon Mews	13 C4	Dell Rd	14 A1	Water La	14 A6
Selborne Rd	13 C6	Dene Path	14 D4	Waterloo St	14 C3
Spenser Rd	13 B2	Dene Rd	14 C3	Watermill Clo	14 A5
Spicers	13 C4	Dunmow Rd	14 D5	Watery La	14 D1
Spitalfields Rd	13 B3	East St	14 C3	Weavers Clo	14 C2
Station Rd	13 C3	Eastern Av	14 C3	Wellesley Rd	14 B5
Stillions Clo	13 C4	Eastfield Clo	14 D3	Wellington Rd	14 A1
Swallow Clo	13 A2	Eastfield Rd	14 C3	Wessex Gdns	14 B2
Tanhouse La	13 B4	Elmbank Rd	14 C4	West St	14 C2
The Butts	13 B6	Eversfield Clo	14 A2	Westbrook Clo	14 C3
The Copperage	13 B4	Farrs Av	14 D4	Western Av	14 B2
The Maltings	13 C5	Forgefield	14 C1	Western Rd	14 B3
The Ridgeway	13 C5	George Yd	14 C3	Weyhill Rd	14 A3
Thorpe Gdns	13 A4	Goddards Mead	14 A4	Whynot La	14 A2
Tilney Clo	13 A4	Halifax Clo	14 A1	Willow Gro	14 A4
Tower St	13 B5	Hanson Rd	14 A1	Winchester Gdns	14 C5
Turk St	13 C4	Heath Vale	14 C4	Winchester Rd	14 C5
Upper Grove Rd	13 C5	Heather Dri	14 B2	Winchester St	14 C3
Vaughans	13 C4	Hedge End Rd	14 D4	Windsor Rd	14 B3
Vicarage Hill	13 B4	Hepworth Clo	14 B1	Winterdyne Mws	14 A3
Vicarage Rd	13 B5	Heron Rise	14 D5	Wolversdene Rd	14 D3
Victoria Rd	13 B3	High St	14 C3	Woodlands Way	14 D3
View Rise	13 A3	Hillside Ct	14 A3	Wyndham Rd	14 A4
Vyne Clo	13 A3	Humberstone Rd	14 C4		
Walnut Clo	13 A3	INDUSTRIAL ESTATES:			
Wentworth Gdns	13 A4	Anton Trading Est	14 B4		

ASHURST

Westbrooke Rd	13 B4	Junction Rd	14 B2		
Whitedown	13 B6	Kings Mdw	14 D3		
Whitedown La	13 A6	Kings Yd	14 C3	Applewood Clo	15 C1
Wickham Clo	13 B6	Lamb Clo	14 D3	Ash Gro	15 C5
Widgeons	13 A2	Lancaster Clo	14 A1	Ash Rd	15 B6
Will Hall Clo	13 A6	Landseer Ct	14 B1	Ashdene Rd	15 B5
William Way	13 B2	Lansdowne Av	14 A4	Ashurst Bridge Rd	15 C2
Willoughby Clo	13 A4	Leicester Pl	14 B3	Ashurst Clo	15 C5
Wilsom Clo	13 C3	Leigh Clo	14 D4	Ashwood Gdns	15 C1
Wilsom Rd	13 C3	Leigh Rd	14 D4	Austen Clo	15 D1
Wincanton Clo	13 C5	Linton Dri	14 B1	Beech Rd	15 B5
Winchester Rd	13 B6	London Rd	14 D3	Birchlands	15 D2
Windmill Hill	13 C4	London St	14 C3	Boakes Pl	15 C5
Windmill La	13 D4	Love La	14 C4	Briarwood Rd	15 C1
Windsor Clo	13 A5	Lowry Ct	14 B1	Bronte Clo	15 D1
Windsor Park	13 C5	Manor Rd	14 A1	Browning Clo	15 D1
Woodland Ct	13 B6	March Clo	14 D1	Busketts Way	15 A6
Wooteys Way	13 A2	Marlborough St	14 C2	Cecil Av	15 C5
Wren Clo	13 B2	Mead Clo	14 A4	Chestnut Dri	15 C4
Yellowhammers	13 A2	Mead Hedges	14 A4	Chillenden Ct	15 D1
York Mews	13 C3	Mead Rd	14 A4	Chiltern Clo	15 D2
Youngs Rd	13 B3	Micheldever Rd	14 D3	Cocklydown La	15 D3

ANDOVER

		Millstream Clo	14 B5	Cooper Rd	15 C5
		Mornington Clo	14 B6	Copinger Clo	15 C1
		Murray Clo	14 B6	Copperfields	15 B1
		Nestor Clo	14 A1	Copsewood Rd	15 C4
		Neville Clo	14 D5	Cyprus Av	15 D5
Acre Ct	14 D3	New St	14 C2	Deerhurst Clo	15 D1
Acre Path	14 D2	Newbury St	14 C2	Deerleap La	15 D4
Adelaide Rd	14 C2	Newcomb Clo	14 B6	Denbigh Clo	15 D2
Alexandra Rd	14 B3	Norman Ct La	14 A6	Dene Rd	15 C5
Andover By-Pass	14 A6	Northern Av	14 B1	Dene Way	15 C1
Anglesey Clo	14 B6	Oakbank Rd	14 C4	Deridene Ct	15 D1
Anton Mill Rd	14 B4	Old Down Rd	14 A1	Dorland Gdns	15 D1
Anton Rd	14 B4	Old Winton Rd	14 C4	Drayton Pl	15 D1
Apsley Clo	14 A6	Osborne Rd	14 B3	Driftwood Gdns	15 C1

Elliot Clo	15 D1	Chequers Rd	16 C3		
Elmtree Clo	15 B5	Chester Pl	16 A4		
Ethelred Gdns	15 C1	Church La	16 B3		
Fastmeare Ct	15 C1	Church Sq	16 B2		
Fir Rd	15 B5	Church St	16 B2		
Fletchwood La	15 A5	Churchill Way	16 B2		
Fletchwood Rd	15 C2	Churchill Way E	16 D2		
Foxhills	15 C3	Churchill Way W	16 A2		
Foxhills Clo	15 C3	Cliddesden Rd	16 C4		
Galsworthy Rd	15 D1	Clifton Ter	16 C2		
Graddidge Way	15 D1	Clifton Walk	16 B2		
Harold Clo	15 D1	Colne Way	16 E3		
Highgrove Clo	15 D3	Constable Clo	16 E4		
Holly Rd	15 B5	Cordale Rd	16 A4		
Hudson Ct	15 B1	Coronation Rd	16 D1		
Hunters Cres	15 B1	Council Rd	16 B4		
Hunters Hill	15 D4	Cromwell Rd	16 B1		
Ibbotson Way	15 D2	Cross St	16 B3		
Itchen Clo	15 D1	Crossborough Gdns	16 D3		
Kayleigh Clo	15 D1	Crossborough Hill	16 D3		
Knellers La	15 D3	Darent Clo	16 D2		
Knightwood Clo	15 C5	Deanes Clo	16 C1		
Lakewood Rd	15 C4	Devonshire Pl	16 A4		
Larchwood Rd	15 C1	Doswell Way	16 C1		
Little Reynolds	15 D2	Downsland Rd	16 A3		
Long Beech Dri	15 D1	Duddon Way	16 E2		
Lyndhurst Rd	15 A6	Eastfield Av	16 D3		
Maple Gdns	15 C1	Eastrop La	16 C2		
Maplewood Clo	15 C1	Eastrop Way	16 D2		
Meredith Gdns	15 D1	Elbow Cnr	16 B2		
Monks Pl	15 D1	Essex Rd	16 A3		
Monkton La	15 D1	Fabian Clo	16 A3		
Myrtle Av	15 D1	Fairfield Ct	16 C4		
New Rd	15 C5	Fairfield Rd	16 B4		
Peregrin Clo	15 C1	Feathers Yd	16 C3		
Peters Croft Av	15 B6	Fencott Pl	16 B1		
Pine Clo	15 C4	Flaxfield Ct	16 B3		
Pipers Clo	15 D1	Flaxfield Rd	16 B3		
Priestlands Clo	15 A1	Francis Rd	16 B4		
Princess Rd	15 B5	Frescade Cres	16 A4		
Redwood Gdns	15 C1	Frome Clo	16 E2		
Reynolds Dale	15 D2	Goat La	16 C3		
Ringwood Rd	15 A1	Gordon Clo	16 D1		
Roundhouse Dri	15 C1	Gresley Rd	16 D1		
Rowan Clo	15 D1	Grove Rd	16 D4		
Rye Dale	15 C4	Hackwood Rd	16 C4		
Serle Gdns	15 D1	Hadleigh Pl	16 B3		
Silkin Gdns	15 D1	Hamble Ct	16 E2		
Surrey Clo	15 D2	Hamelyn Clo	16 A4		
Swallow Clo	15 C1	Hamelyn Rd	16 A4		
Tamorisk Dri	15 C1	Hammond Rd	16 A4		
The Cleeves	15 D1	Hardy La	16 A4		
The Dorrits	15 B1	Hawkfield La	16 A4		
Thomas Clo	15 D1	Heath Clo	16 E2		
Timpson Clo	15 C1	Hogarth Clo	16 F3		
Totton Western By-Pass	15 C4	Holbein Clo	16 E4		
Whartons Clo	15 C4	Hollins Walk	16 C2		
Whartons La	15 C4	INDUSTRIAL ESTATES:			
Wingrove Rd	15 C4	Eastrop Business Area	16 D2		
Wood Rd	15 C5	Irwell Clo	16 D3		
Woodlands Drove	15 A5	Jacobs Yd	16 C3		
Woodlands Rd	15 A5	Joices Yd	16 B3		
Woodside Gdns	15 C4	Jubilee Rd	16 B4		

BASINGSTOKE

		Kennet Clo	16 E3	
Albert Yd	16 B3	Kingsclere Rd	16 A1	
Alencon Link	16 B2	Lancaster Rd	16 A1	
Alexandra Rd	16 A3	Lea Clo	16 E2	
Allnut Av	16 D3	Loddon Dri	16 D2	
Anchor Yd	16 B2	Loddon Mall	16 B2	
Applegarth Clo	16 C4	London Rd	16 C3	
Arun Ct	16 E2	Longcraft Clo	16 A3	
Avon Walk	16 E2	Longmoor Rd	16 A3	
Basing Rd	16 F1	Lower Brook St	16 A2	
Basing Vw	16 C2	Lower Wote St	16 C2	
Beaconsfield Rd	16 D2	Lune Ct	16 E2	
Beaulieu Ct	16 D2	Lyford Rd	16 C1	
Bedford Walk	16 E3	Lyn Ct	16 E2	
Black Dam Way	16 F3	Lytton Rd	16 D3	
Blackwater Clo	16 D2	Mark La	16 C3	
Blair Clo	16 A4	Market Pl	16 C3	
Bounty Rise	16 B4	May Pl	16 C3	
Bounty Road	16 A4	May St	16 A2	
Bourne Ct	16 E2	Medway Ct	16 E2	
Bowyer Clo	16 A4	Meon Walk	16 E2	
Bramblys Clo	16 B3	Merton Rd	16 A1	
Bramblys Dri	16 A3	Montague Pl	16 C4	
Brookvale Ct	16 A2	Mortimer La	16 B3	
Budds Clo	16 A3	New Mkt Sq	16 C2	
Bunnian Pl	16 C2	New Rd	16 C2	
Burgess Rd	16 B1	New St	16 B3	
Cam Walk	16 E3	Norden Clo	16 C1	
Castle Rd	16 A4	Norn Hill	16 D1	
Castle Sq	16 B2	Norn Hill Clo	16 D1	
Castons Yd	16 B2	Old Basing Mall	16 B2	
Chapel Hill	16 B1	Old Reading Rd	16 B2	
Chelmer Ct	16 D2	Padwick Clo	16 A4	
		Park Gdns	16 D4	
		Parkside Rd	16 D4	
		Penrith Rd	16 A4	
		Phoenix Pk Ter	16 B1	

Pittard Rd	16 A4
Porchester Sq	16 C2
Potters Walk	16 C3
Queen Annes Walk	16 C3
Queen Mary Av	16 B1
Queens Rd	16 A2
Raphael Clo	16 F4
Rayleigh Rd	16 A3
Red Lion La	16 C3
Rembrandt Clo	16 E4
Renoir Clo	16 E4
Reynolds Clo	16 F4
Ribble Way	16 E2
Richmond Rd	16 B1
Ringway East	16 E1
Ringway South	16 D4
Rochford Rd	16 A3
Roding Clo	16 D2
Rothay Ct	16 E2
Roundmead Rd	16 A3
Ruskin Clo	16 F4
St Johns Walk	16 B2
St Marys Ct	16 C2
Sarum Hill	16 A3
Seal Rd	16 C3
Severn Way	16 E3
Sherborne Rd	16 A1
Shooters Way	16 C1
Simmons Walk	16 E3
Solbys Rd	16 A3
Soper Gro	16 B1
Southend Rd	16 A2
Southern Rd	16 C3
Station App	16 B1
Station Hill	16 B2
Station Mall	16 B2
Stukley Rd	16 A3
Sylvia Clo	16 B4
Test Way	16 E2
Thames Ct	16 E2
The Danes	16 C2
The Glebe	16 B2
The Laurels	16 D1
Timberlake Rd	16 B2
Trent Way	16 E2
Turner Clo	16 F3
Van Dyck Clo	16 F4
Victoria St	16 B3
Vyne Road	16 B1
Wallis Rd	16 B4
Warton Rd	16 D1
Weale Ct	16 B1
Wesley Walk	16 C2
Wessex Clo	16 A4
Weysprings Clo	16 E2
Whistler Clo	16 E4
White Hart La	16 D3
Winchcombe Rd	16 A3
Winchester Rd	16 A4
Winchester St	16 B3
Windrush Clo	16 E3
Winterthor Way	16 B2
Winton Sq	16 B3
Worting Rd	16 A3
Wote St	16 C3

BISHOPS WALTHAM

Albany Ct	17 A2
Albany Dri	17 A2
Albany Rd	17 A2
Albert Rd	17 C3
Andrewes Clo	17 D2
Ashton Clo	17 A1
Bank St	17 E2
Basingwell St	17 E3
Battery Hill	17 B2
Beaufort Dri	17 D2
Beeches La	17 E1
Bishops La	17 D3
Blanchard Rd	17 C2
Botley Rd	17 D4
Brook St	17 D3
Brooklands Rd	17 D2
Butts Farm La	17 F2
Chalky La	17 F1
Cherry Gdns	17 F3
Churchill Av	17 A1
Claylands Ct	17 B2
Claylands Rd	17 C2
Colville Dri	17 F2
Coppice Hill	17 E3
Corn Hill	17 F1
Cricklemead	17 F3
Cross St	17 E3
Cunningham Av	17 B2
Denewulfe Clo	17 D2
Dundridge La	17 F1
Eastways	17 E3
Edington Clo	17 C2
Elizabeth Way	17 C3
Elm Rd	17 F2
Folly Field	17 E3
Free St	17 E2
Garfield Clo	17 D2
Garfield Rd	17 D2
Green La	17 F3
Greens Clo	17 C2
Hall Clo	17 F2
Hamble Springs	17 F3
Hermitage Clo	17 B1
High St	17 E3
Hoe Rd	17 F3
Houchin St	17 E3
Kestrel Clo	17 B2
Langton Rd	17 D2
Leopold Dri	17 B3
Little Shore La	17 E3
Lower La	17 E2
Mallard Clo	17 B2
Malt La	17 D3
Malvern Clo	17 E3
Marlow Rd	17 B1
Martin St	17 C3
Merlin Clo	17 C2
Middle Brook	17 E2
Middle St	17 E3
Morley Dri	17 D2
Northfields Clo	17 B1
Oak Rd	17 F2
Park Rd	17 B2
Penfords Paddock	17 F3
Pine Rd	17 F3
Pondside La	17 C2
Princes Clo	17 C2
Priory Clo	17 C2
Rareridge La	17 F2
Red Lion St	17 E3
St Bonnet Dri	17 D2
St George Sq	17 D3
St Peters St	17 E3
St Swithins Clo	17 C2
Shore Cres	17 E3
Shore La	17 E3
Siskin Clo	17 A2
Southfields Clo	17 D3
Station Rd	17 D3
Tangier La	17 A3
Tennyson Clo	17 F2
The Avenue	17 B3
The Hawthorns	17 B1
The Priory	17 C3
Victoria Rd	17 C2
Waynflete Clo	17 D2
Willow Rd	17 F3
Winchester	17 A1

BROCKENHURST

Addison Rd	18 C5
Armstrong Clo	18 B3
Armstrong La	18 B3
Armstrong Rd	18 B3
Auckland Av	18 C4
Auckland Pl	18 C4
Avenue Rd	18 C4
Back La	18 D4
Balmer Lawn Rd	18 D1
Broadlands Rd	18 A2
Brookley Rd	18 C3
Brookside Rd	18 C3
Burford La	18 C2
Burley Rd	18 A4
Butts Lawn	18 C2
Careys Cotts	18 C2
Chestnut Rd	18 C3
Church La	18 D4
Collyers Rd	18 C5
Culverley Clo	18 C4
East Bank Rd	18 C4
Fathersfield	18 C3
Fibbards Rd	18 C3
Forest Glade Clo	18 A3
Forest Hall	18 D3
Forest Pk Rd	18 B2
Forest View	18 A3
Greenways Rd	18 D3
Grigg La	18 C3
Highwood Rd	18 C4
Horlock Rd	18 C3
Knowle Rd	18 A3
Lymington Rd	18 D6
Lyndhurst Rd	18 D1
Martins Rd	18 C2
Meadow End	18 B3
Meerut Rd	18 B2
Mill La	18 D4
Moorlands Clo	18 A3
New Forest Dri	18 A2
Noel Clo	18 D3
North Rd	18 D3
North Weirs	18 A4
Ober Rd	18 B3
Oberfield Rd	18 A2
Park Clo	18 C2
Partridge Rd	18 C4
Rhinefield Clo	18 B3
Rhinefield Rd	18 A2
South Weirs	18 A5
Sutton Pl	18 D3
Sway Rd	18 B6
Tattenham Rd	18 C4
The Coppice	18 A3
The Paddock	18 C3
The Rise	18 C3
Tilebarn La	18 C6
Waters Grn	18 D3
Waters Green Ct	18 D3
Whitemoor Rd	18 A3
Widelane Clo	18 C3
Wilverley Rd	18 B3
Woodlands Rd	18 C5

COSHAM

Ackworth Rd	19 D6
Albert Rd	19 C3
Aldroke St	19 C3
Allaway Av	19 A2
Arran Clo	19 C2
*Ashley Walk, Windsor Rd	19 C4
Ashurst Rd	19 B3
Bapaume Rd	19 C6
Beaconsfield Av	19 D4
Bell Rd	19 A3
Bernard Av	19 D3
Blackwater Clo	19 A3
Blakemere Cres	19 A1
Boston Rd	19 B2
Braintree Rd	19 A2
Bredenbury Cres	19 A1
Brighstone Rd	19 B3
Bromyard Cres	19 A2
Bryson Rd	19 A3
Burrill Av	19 D3
Carronade Walk	19 C6
Cavell Dri	19 B2
Chalkridge Rd	19 D2
Chatsworth Av	19 C4
Cheltenham Rd	19 A3
Chidham Rd	19 D2
Chipstead Rd	19 C3
Clacton Rd	19 A2
Colchester Rd	19 B2
Colville Rd	19 D2
Colwell Rd	19 C4
Copnor Rd	19 C6
Cosham Park Av	19 C4
Court La	19 D4
Courtmount Gro	19 D2
Courtmount Path	19 D2
Cow La	19 B3
Cranborne Rd	19 D2
Cromer Rd	19 B2
Curie Rd	19 B2
Deal Rd	19 B2
Dean Rd	19 C3
Dersingham Clo	19 B2
Donaldson Rd	19 C5
Dorking Cres	19 C3
Dorstone Rd	19 A1
Dovercourt Rd	19 D5
Dursley Cres	19 A3
East Cosham Rd	19 D2
East Ct	19 D3
Edgerley Gdns	19 C5
Elgin Rd	19 C5
Fairfield Sq	19 B2
Falklands Rd	19 B6
Farmside Gdns	19 C6
Fawley Rd	19 B6
Feltons Pl	19 C6
Fifth Av	19 B3
Firgrove Cres	19 C5
First Av	19 C3
Fitzpatrick Ct	19 A2
Fourth Av	19 B3
Freshwater Rd	19 B3
Glebefield Gdns	19 B3
Glenleigh Av	19 C3
Greenwood Av	19 A3
Gunstore Rd	19 D6
Gurnard Rd	19 B3
Hadleigh Rd	19 A2
Halstead Rd	19 A3
Harleston Rd	19 A1
Harvey Rd	19 B2
Harwich Rd	19 A2
Havant Rd	19 C3
Hawthorn Cres	19 C4
Herne Rd	19 B3
High St	19 C3
Highbury Gro	19 C4
Highbury Way	19 C4
Hilary Av	19 D3
Hilsea Cres	19 B6
Hockley Clo	19 B2
Holbeach Clo	19 B2
Horsea La	19 A6
Horsea Rd	19 B6
Howard Rd	19 B6
Hunter Rd	19 C2
Hythe Rd	19 B2
INDUSTRIAL ESTATES:	
Acorn Business Centre	19 A3
Islay Gdns	19 C2
Jasmond Rd	19 C5
Jenner Rd	19 C2
Jura Clo	19 C2
Kintyre Rd	19 C2
Knowsley Cres	19 D4
Knowsley Rd	19 C4
Langdale Av	19 D4
Lendorber Av	19 D3
Limberline Rd	19 D6
Limberline Spur	19 D6
Lindisfarne Clo	19 D3
Lister Rd	19 B2
Lodge Av	19 D3
London Rd	19 C2
Lonsdale Av	19 D4
Lowestoft Rd	19 A2
Ludlow Rd	19 A2
Mablethorpe Rd	19 B1
Magdala Rd	19 C3
Maidstone Cres	19 B2
Maldon Rd	19 A2
Mallow Clo	19 C3
Matapan Rd	19 A6
Medina Rd	19 A3
Mellor Clo	19 A2
Midway Rd	19 B6
Military Rd	19 A1
Military Rd, Hilsea	19 C5
Mill La	19 B1
Mulberry Av	19 D3
Mulberry La	19 D3
Mulberry Path	19 D3
New Down La	19 D1
North Av	19 B6
Northarbour Path	19 A3
Northarbour Rd	19 A3
Northarbour Spur	19 A3
Northern Par	19 B6
Northern Rd	19 C4
Northwood Rd	19 B6
Norway Rd	19 C6
Norwich Rd	19 A2
Oakwood Rd	19 B6
Old London Rd	19 C6
Old Wymering Rd	19 B3
Orkney Rd	19 C2
Padwick Av	19 D3
Pangbourne Av	19 D4
Park Gro	19 C4
Park La	19 D3
Parr Rd	19 A3
Parsons Clo	19 C6
Pasteur Rd	19 B2
Pebmarsh Rd	19 B3
Peronne Clo	19 C6
Peronne Rd	19 C6
Pervin Rd	19 C3
Peterborough Rd	19 B2
Pigeon House La	19 A1
Pitreavie Rd	19 C5
Portsdown Hill Rd	19 B1
Portsmouth Rd	19 C4
Portswood Rd	19 B6
Rampart Gdns	19 C5
Regal Clo	19 C3
Rochford Rd	19 A2
Roebuck Clo	19 C4
Rosebery Av	19 D4
St Colmans Av	19 D3
St Georges Rd	19 C3
St Johns Rd	19 C2
St Matthews Rd	19 C3
Salisbury Rd	19 D4
Sandown Rd	19 B3
Scott Rd	19 C6
Second Av	19 B3
Sevenoaks Rd	19 B2
Sheringham Rd	19 A1
Shetland Clo	19 C2
Simpson Rd	19 C2
Sixth Av	19 B3
South Av	19 B6
Southampton Rd	19 A3
Southdown Rd	19 D2
Southwick Hill Rd	19 A1
Spur Rd	19 C3
Stamshaw Prom	19 A6
Stanford Clo	19 A2
Sudbury Rd	19 A2
Sundridge Clo	19 C3
Tankerton Clo	19 B2
Tewkesbury Clo	19 A2
The Close	19 D3
The Droke	19 C3
The Old Road	19 C4
The Orchard	19 C4
Third Av	19 B3
Totland Rd	19 B3
Tudor Cres	19 C5
Tunstall Rd	19 A2
Vectis Way	19 C3
Walberton Av	19 D3
Walsingham Clo	19 A2
Washbrook Rd	19 A2
Wayte St	19 C3
Wembley Gro	19 D5
Westerham Clo	19 B2
Western Rd	19 A3
Whippingham Clo	19 A3
Whitstable Rd	19 B2
Widley Court Dri	19 D3
Widley Rd	19 D2
Widley Walk	19 C1
Willersley Clo	19 A2
Windsor Rd	19 C4
Winterhill Rd	19 A3
Woolner Av	19 D3
Wooton St	19 C3
Wymering La	19 B2
Wymering Manor Clo	19 B3
York Ter	19 C6

COWPLAIN

Acacia Gdns	20 D3
Acres La	20 D6
Aintree Dri	20 C6
Almond Clo	20 D3
Anvil Clo	20 D6
Ash Clo	20 A5
Ash Copse	20 B2
Ashington Clo	20 C4
Ashley Clo	20 A2
Aspen Way	20 B3
Barton Cross	20 C1
Beech Clo	20 B6
Beech Way	20 D3
Benbow Clo	20 D1
Bevan Rd	20 B3
Birch Clo	20 A5
Birdlip Clo	20 C2
Blackbird Clo	20 B3
Blenheim Rd	20 C2
Bourne Clo	20 D1
Bowers Clo	20 C3
Bowes-Lyon Ct	20 D1
Brewster Clo	20 C4
Briar Clo	20 D2
Briarfield Gdns	20 C2
Bulls Copse La	20 C2
Bunting Gdns	20 A4
Catherington La	20 C1
Causeway Farm	20 C2
Cedar Cres	20 D2
Celandine Av	20 D4
Chaffinch Grn	20 A3
Chatburn Av	20 A5
Chaucer Clo	20 A6
Chepstow Ct	20 D6
Cheriton Clo	20 C1
Cherry Tree Av	20 D5
Chesterton Gdns	20 A4
Chestnut Av	20 D3
Churchill Ct	20 C2
Coldhill La	20 A1
Coleridge Gdns	20 B3
Conifer Clo	20 C5
Cornbrook Gro	20 D6
Cotwell Av	20 C4
Crestland Clo	20 C4
Cricket Dri	20 B2
Crisspyn Clo	20 D2
Crombie Clo	20 B3
Cross La	20 C2

Inner By-Pass	22 D5
King St	22 D5
Kings Rd	22 C6
Kings Ter	22 D5
Kingsley Av	22 C5
Kinnel Clo	22 C5
Lane End Dri	22 C5
Laurence Grn	22 D2
Lewis Rd	22 D2
Linden Clo	22 C3
Lisle Way	22 C2
Long Copse Rd	22 C1
Longfield Rd	22 C2
Lumley Rd	22 D5
Lutmain St	22 C2
Maismore Gdns	22 B6
Maple Clo	22 D3
Marina Clo	22 D6
Markway Clo	22 B5
Marlborough Pk	22 A3
Meadow Ct	22 D5
Neville Gdns	22 C2
New Brighton Rd	22 D4
Nile St	22 D5
Nore Cres	22 B4
Nore Farm Av	22 B4
North St	22 D4
Nursery Clo	22 D2
Oak Meadow	22 D2
Oak Tree Dri	22 C1
Orange Row	22 D6
Palmers Rd	22 D5
Panton Clo	22 C2
Park Cres	22 B5
Pelham Ter	22 D5
Queen St	22 D6
Racton Rd	22 D2
Record Rd	22 C5
Redlands La	22 D2
Rowan Rd	22 A2
St James Rd	22 D5
St Peters Sq	22 D6
School La	22 D5
Seafields	22 C6
Seagull La	22 D5
Selangor Av	22 A5
Silvertrees	22 D3
South St	22 D6
Southleigh Rd	22 A2
Spencer Rd	22 C2
Spindle Clo	22 A3
Spindle Warren	22 A3
Spring Gdns	22 D5
Stanley Rd	22 D6
Sultan Rd	22 D4
Swan Clo	22 D6
The Fishermans	22 D6
The Greenway	22 C2
The Promenade	22 D6
The Rookery	22 D5
Tower St	22 D6
Tudor Av	22 C2
Valetta Pk	22 C6
Victoria Rd	22 B4
Wallrock Walk	22 C2
Warblington Rd	22 C6
Wards Cres	22 D3
Washington Rd	22 C4
Watersedge Gdns	22 C6
Weavers Grn	22 A3
Wensley Gdns	22 D3
West Rd	22 B6
West St	22 D4
Westbourne Av	22 D4
Westbourne Clo	22 D4
Western Av	22 B5
Western Parade	22 D5
Westgrove Gdns	22 D5
Whittington Ct	22 C5
Wickor Clo	22 D3
Wickor Way	22 D2
Winfield Way	22 D2
Woodlands Av	22 D4
Woodroofe Walk	22 D2
Woolmer St	22 C2
Wraysbury Dri	22 D1
Wraysbury Pk	22 D1

FAREHAM

Adelaide Pl	23 C5
Alexander Gro	23 B6
Archery La	23 C4
Arundel Dri	23 A4
Avenue Rd	23 A5
Bath La	23 C5
Beaconsfield Rd	23 B6
Beaufort Av	23 A3
Belvoir Clo	23 B5
Bentley Cres	23 A3
Briarwood Clo	23 B5
Bridge Foot Dri	23 D4
Broadcut	23 C3
Bruce Clo	23 A3
Burnham Wood	23 A2
Byron Clo	23 A3
Cawtes Pl	23 C4
Chamberlain Gro	23 A6
Charlemount Dri	23 D4
Chaucer Clo	23 A4
Church Pl	23 C4
Church Pth	23 C4
Civic Way	23 C4
Coghlan Clo	23 B4
Colenso Rd	23 D4
Compass Point	23 B5
Coome Farm Av	23 B5
Cornfield	23 B2
Crawford Dri	23 A2
Crescent Rd	23 B5
Deanes Park Rd	23 D5
Delme Dri	23 D4
Denbigh Dri	23 A3
Derlyn Rd	23 B4
Drift Rd	23 D3
Dryden Clo	23 A4
Earls Rd	23 B6
East Hill Clo	23 D4
East St	23 C5
Eastern Parade	23 C6
Eastern Way	23 C5
Eden Rise	23 B5
Elmhurst Rd	23 B5
Elms Rd	23 B6
Fayre Rd	23 B6
Foxgloves	23 C2
Furneaux Gdns	23 B2
Furzehall Av	23 B2
Giles Clo	23 B2
Gordon Rd	23 A4
Gosport Rd	23 B6
Greenbanks Gdns	23 D4
Greenwood Clo	23 B2
Grove Rd	23 A4
Gudge Heath La	23 A4
Hanover Gdns	23 B2
Harebell Clo	23 C2
Harrison Rd	23 B3
Hartlands Rd	23 B5
Hickley Path	23 D4
High St	23 C4
Highfield Av	23 A6
Holbrook Rd	23 B5
INDUSTRIAL ESTATES:	
Bridge Ind Est	23 D3
Fareham Ind Park	23 D3
Irvine Clo	23 A2
Johns Rd	23 B6
Kiln Acre	23 B2
Kiln Rd	23 A2
Kings Rd	23 B5
Kneller Ct	23 A2
Leigh Rd	23 A4
Longstaffe Gdns	23 A2
Lower Quay	23 C6
Lower Quay Clo	23 C6
Lysses Ct	23 C4
Lysses Path	23 C4
Maddison Ct	23 C5
Mallory Cres	23 A3
Malthouse La	23 B4
Maylings Farm Rd	23 A3
Maytree Gdns	23 A5
Maytree Rd	23 A5
Mead Way	23 B3
Military Rd	23 D3
Mill Rd	23 B6
Miller Dri	23 A3
Morshead Cres	23 A3
New Rd	23 B4
Nine Elms La	23 D1
North Hill	23 B2
North Wallington	23 D3
Northwood Sq	23 B4
Norton Dri	23 A3
Old Gosport Rd	23 B6
Old Turnpike	23 B2
Osborn Rd	23 B4
Osborn Road Sth	23 B4
Oxford Clo	23 A3
Pallant Gdns	23 D4
Palmerston Av	23 C4
Park La	23 B4
Paxton St	23 A5
Pinks Hill	23 D4
Pook La	23 B1
Portland St	23 C5
Potters Av	23 A2
Poyner Clo	23 B4
Quay St	23 C5
Queens Rd	23 B5
Radclyffe Rd	23 D3
Redlands La	23 A5
Riverside Av	23 D3
Russell Rd	23 B4
St Annes Gro	23 A6
St Christopher Av	23 C3
St Michaels Gro	23 A6
St Sebastian Cres	23 C3
St Thomas Clo	23 C3
Salterns	23 C6
Saville Gdns	23 A2
Seabird Way	23 B3
Serpentine Rd	23 B3
Somervell Dri	23 A3
Southampton Rd	23 B4
Spurlings Rd	23 D1
Standard Way	23 D2
Stephen Rd	23 A4
Swallow Wood	23 B2
Tangle Wood	23 B2
Tennyson Gdns	23 A4
Tensing Clo	23 A2
The Avenue	23 A5
The Drive	23 A4
The Gillies	23 A5
The Heights	23 D3
The Mallards	23 B2
The Maltings	23 D3
The Meadows	23 C2
The Potteries	23 C3
Trinity Gdns	23 B4
Trinity St	23 B4
Union St	23 C4
Uplands Cres	23 B3
Upper St Michaels Gro	23 A6
Upper Wharf	23 C5
Wakefield Rd	23 A2
Wallington Hill	23 C4
Wallington Shore Rd	23 D4
Wallington Way	23 D4
Wallisdean Av	23 A5
Waterside Gdns	23 D4
West Downs Clo	23 B2
West St	23 B4
Westborn Rd	23 B4
Westbury Rd	23 B4
Western Rd	23 B5
Western Way	23 A5
Westfield Av	23 A6
Westley Gro	23 A5
Wickham Rd	23 B1
William Price Gdns	23 B4
Woodlands	23 D4
Young Bridge Ct	23 B6

FARNBOROUGH

Abbey Way	24 B2
Adlington Pl	24 C3
Aircraft Esp	24 B5
Albert Rd	24 B4
Alexandra Ct	24 B5
Alexandra Rd	24 B4
Andrewartha Rd	24 C4
Artillery Rd	24 C6
Ashdown Av	24 C3
Ashley Rd	24 C2
Avenue Rd	24 B2
Barnes Clo	24 C2
Belvedere Rd	24 B4
Blackwater Valley Rd	24 C2
Blaise Clo	24 C2
Blenheim Ct	24 C3
Blenheim Rd	24 A6
Boundary Rd	24 B4
Briarlees Ct	24 C6
Broadlands	24 D3
Brookwood Rd	24 C2
Bruntile Clo	24 C5
Buller Ct	24 B5
Cambridge Rd E	24 B5
Cambridge Rd W	24 B5
Camp Rd	24 B6
Canterbury Rd	24 C4
Carlyon Clo	24 B2
Cedar Rd	24 B3
Chalfont Dri	24 B4
Charlcote Clo	24 C3
Church Path	24 B2
Church Path	24 B6
Church Rd E	24 B4
Church Rd W	24 B4
Clandon Ct	24 C3
Clevedon Ct	24 C3
Clockhouse Rd	24 A2
Closeworth Rd	24 C6
Coleford Bridge Rd	24 C1
Collingwood	24 D5
Cropleigh Ct	24 A2
Cross St	24 A5
Cunnington Rd	24 C4
Douai Clo	24 B2
East Mead	24 A2
Eldergrove	24 D5
Elles Clo	24 A3
Elles Rd	24 A3
Elm Grove Rd	24 A2
Farnborough Rd	24 A1
Fellows Rd	24 C5
Firgrove Ct	24 A2
Firgrove Par	24 A2
Firs Clo	24 B4
Gainsborough Clo	24 B4
Goodwood Pl	24 C3
Gordon Rd	24 A4
Government House Rd	24 A6
Gravel Rd	24 C6
Green Croft	24 A2
Guildford Rd	24 B5
Hamesmoor Rd	24 D2
Hamesmoor Way	24 D2
Hatfield Gdns	24 C3
Helen Ct	24 A2
Hermitage Clo	24 C5
High St	24 B6
High View Rd	24 A2
Highgate La	24 B1
Hilder Gdns	24 C3
Hollybush La	24 D6
I.A.M. Rd	24 A6
*Institute Rd, Redvers Buller Rd	24 B6
Jubilee Hall Rd	24 B6
Kingsmead	24 A2
Leopold Av	24 A1
Longleat Sq	24 C3
Lynchford La	24 D5
Lynchford Rd	24 A6
Maitland Rd	24 A6
Manor Rd	24 C2
Mathews Clo	24 C6
Meudon Av	24 A3
Monks Clo	24 B2
Montacute Rd	24 C2
Morris Rd	24 C6
Netley St	24 A6
North Gate	24 B4
North Rd	24 B6
Northmead	24 A2
Oak Rd	24 B3
Old Rectory Gdns	24 C2
Osborne Rd	24 B5
Oxford Rd	24 B4
Parish Rd	24 A6
Park Rd	24 D5
Peabody Rd	24 B5
Pennswood	24 C4
Pierrefondes Av	24 A1
Pinehurst Av	24 A3
Pirbright Rd	24 B3
Princes Mead	24 A2
Priory St	24 C1
Queen Victoria Ct	24 A1
Queens Av	24 B6
Queens Clo	24 A6
Queens Ct	24 B6
Queens Rd	24 B6
Queensmead	24 A2
Quinneys	24 B4
R.A.E. Rd	24 B4
Rapallo Clo	24 B2
Reading Rd	24 B5
Rectory Rd	24 B2
Redvers Buller Rd	24 B6
Rivers Clo	24 C5
St Marks Clo	24 B5
Salesian Vw	24 D6
Salisbury Rd	24 B2
Saltram Rd	24 B5
Sarah Way	24 A2
Sherborne Rd	24 C5
Solartron Rd	24 A3
Somerset Rd	24 B5
South St	24 D5
Southampton St	24 A6
Stable Clo	24 A2
Station App	24 A1
Station Rd	24 A2
Stourhead Clo	24 C2
Sullivan Clo	24 A1
Sycamore Rd	24 B3
Syon Pl	24 C2
Talgarth Dri	24 C2
The Crescent	24 B3
The Grove	24 C4
The Mead	24 A2
The Sycamores	24 C3
Tredenham Clo	24 B6
Tregolls Dri	24 B2
Union St	24 A2
Upton Clo	24 C3
Victoria Rd	24 A2
Virginia Gdns	24 B3
Waverley Rd	24 C3
Westmead	24 A2
Wetherby Gdns	24 B5
Whiteacre Rd	24 D2
Whites Rd	24 D5
Willow Clo	24 D2
Wilton Ct	24 C3
Winchester St	24 B6
Windsor Rd	24 C5
Woburn Av	24 C2
Wymering Rd	24 C3
Yeovil Rd	24 C5
Yetminster Rd	24 C5
York Rd	24 B5

FAWLEY

A Avenue	25 A2
Admirals Clo	25 D1
Ashdown	25 B3
Ashdown Rd	25 B3
Ashlett Clo	25 D1
Ashlett Mews	25 D2
Ashlett Rd	25 D2
B Avenue	25 A2
Bell Clo	25 B4
Bernwood Gro	25 B6
Bevis Clo	25 B3
Blackfield Rd	25 A4
Bowland Way	25 B6
C Avenue	25 A1
Calshot Rd	25 D2
Cedric Clo	25 C5
Chalewood Rd	25 B6
Chapel La, Blackfield	25 B6
Chapel La, Fawley	25 B2
Charlesley Ct	25 C2
Charnwood Way	24 A6
Church La	25 C2
Churchfields	25 C1
Clare Gdns	25 C6
Colville Av	25 C2
Copthorne La	25 D1
D Avenue	25 A1
Dane Clo	25 B5
Dark La	25 B4
Denny	25 B1
Dunfield Way	25 B3
Edward Clo	25 B5
Exbury Rd	25 A5
Falcon Fields	25 C2
Fawley By Pass	25 C2
Fawley Rd	25 A3
Fields Clo	25 A5
Fifth St	25 A1
First St	25 B1
Forest Edge	25 C2
Forest Gate	25 C6
Forge Rd	25 C6
Forrester Rd	25 B4
Four Shells Rd	25 B4
Fourth St	25 A1
Foxhayes La	25 C6
Foxlands	25 C6
Foxs Glade	25 C6
Foxs Walk	25 C6
Foxy Paddock	25 C6
Fry Clo	25 B3
Furzey Clo	25 B4
Gatewood Clo	25 B6
Glyn Jones Rd	25 B4
Green La	25 C5
Hampton Clo	25 B5
Hampton Gdns	25 B5
Hampton La	25 A4
Hartsgrove Av	25 B5
Hartsgrove Clo	25 B5
Harvey Ct	25 A4
Heather Rd	25 B4
Hedley Clo	25 B4
Holly Rd	25 B6
Hursley Dri	25 B6
Janes Clo	25 B5

Kings Copse Rd	25 A5	Bransome Rd	26 A1
Kings Ride	25 B6	Brinksway	26 B3
Langley Lodge Gdns	25 C6	Brook Clo	26 B3
Lea Rd	25 B6	Brookly Gdns	26 C1
Lepe Rd	25 B6	Broom Acres	26 B5
Lightning Clo	25 B3	Bryanstone Clo	26 C5
Linda Rd	25 C1	Burns Av	26 D5
Long Copse	25 A3	Burnside	26 B2
Marsh La	25 C1	Byron Clo	26 B3
Meadow Way	25 C2	Camden Walk	26 D2
Milleken Clo	25 B3	Campbell Clo	26 A2
Mopley	25 B6	Carlton Cres	26 C5
Mopley Clo	25 B6	Carthona Dri	26 B3
New Rd	25 B5	Castle St	26 B4
Newlands Clo	25 B5	Castor Ct	26 D5
Newlands Copse	25 B4	Cavendish Gdns	26 A6
Newlands Rd	25 A3	Champion Way	26 B6
Nicholas Rd	25 B6	Chesilton Cres	26 B6
Norman Rd	25 B5	Chestnut Gro	26 C1
Northampton La	25 B5	Chiltern Clo	26 C5
Orchard Clo	25 C2	Chinnock Clo	26 A4
Pendleton Gdns	25 A4	Church Ct	26 B2
Priestcroft Dri	25 A4	Church Gro	26 A2
*Richards Clo,		Church Rd	26 B2
Heather Rd	25 B6	Clarence Rd	26 B3
Rye Paddock La	25 C1	Compton Clo	26 C6
Rhyme Hall Mews	25 D2	Compton Rd	26 C6
St Francis Clo	25 B6	Conifer Clo	26 B6
St Francis Rd	25 B6	Coniston Way	26 A6
St Michaels Clo	25 B4	Connaught Rd	26 B3
Salterns La	25 C1	Coombe Dri	26 D2
Saxon Rd	25 B5	Copse La	26 A6
School Rd	25 C2	Corringway	26 C5
Second St	25 B1	Court Moor Av	26 B4
Sharingham Clo	25 C1	Coxheath Rd	26 A6
Sherwood Way	25 B6	Coxmoor Clo	26 D6
Slades Hill	25 B3	Cranford Av	26 A6
Smith Clo	25 B3	Crookham Rd	26 A4
South Av	25 A3	Crown Gdns	26 C3
Stag Gates	25 A5	Curtis Ct	26 B5
Stonehills	25 D2	Darset Av	26 C1
The Drove	25 A5	Denman Clo	26 D2
The Fowey	25 A4	Denning Clo	26 A4
The Glade	25 B6	Dinorben Av	26 A4
The Greenwich	25 A4	Dinorben Beeches	26 A3
The Lane	25 C2	Dinorben Clo	26 A4
The Paddocks	25 C2	Dudley Ct	26 B5
The Pentagon	25 B3	Dunmow Hill	26 C1
The Square	25 C2	Durnsford Av	26 B4
Third St	25 A1	Edney Clo	26 D5
Thornbury Av	25 B5	Elizabeth Dri	26 B6
Thornhill Clo	25 B3	Elms Rd	26 D2
Thornhill Rd	25 B3	Fairland Clo	26 C3
Toomer Clo	25 B3	Fairmile	26 B5
Valley Clo	25 B4	Ferbies	26 B5
Viking Clo	25 B5	Fern Dri	26 A5
Walkers Lane Nth	25 B5	Ferndale Rd	26 A6
Walkers Lane Sth	25 C6	Fir Clo	26 A3
Walverley Pl	25 A4	Fir Tree Way	26 D3
Wessex Clo	25 B5	Firethorn Clo	26 B4
West Common Rd	25 B6	Fleet Rd	26 A3
Wheelers Walk	25 B5	Florence Rd	26 C5
Whites La	25 D1	Folly Clo	26 C4
Woodville Av	25 C2	Forest End	26 A5
Wynchwood Dri	25 B6	Foxcroft	26 C6

FLEET

Abbots Clo	26 B2	Foye La	26 C6
Adams Dri	26 D2	Frensham Av	26 D2
Albany Clo	26 C3	Fugelmere Rd	26 D1
Albany Rd	26 B3	Fugelmere Walk	26 D1
Albert St	26 A3	Gally Hill Rd	26 A6
Aldershot Rd,		George Rd	26 C2
Church Crookham	26 C6	Glebe Ct	26 A2
Aldershot Rd, Fleet	26 B3	Glen Rd	26 A3
Alton Rd	26 D2	Gordon Av	26 B3
Andrew Clo	26 B5	Gorseway	26 C4
Annes Way	26 C5	Gough Rd	26 A1
Arundel Clo	26 C3	Grange Est	26 A6
Avenue Rd	26 A1	Grange Rd	26 A6
Avondale Rd	26 C1	Grantley Dri	26 A4
Award Rd	26 B6	Gravel Rd	26 C5
Azalea Gdns	26 C6	Greenleys	26 A6
Barbara Clo	26 C5	Greenways	26 A5
Barbary Clo	26 B4	Grove Rd	26 D6
Basingbourne Clo	26 B5	Guildford Rd	26 C6
Basingbourne Rd	26 B5	Haig La	26 C6
Beacon Hill Rd	26 D6	Hamilton Way	26 C5
Bearwood Clo	26 B2	Harlington Way	26 A2
Beaufort Rd	26 C4	Hartsleaf Clo	26 B3
Beech Ride	26 A4	Hawkins Way	26 D3
Berkeley Clo	26 C2	Haywood Dri	26 B4
Birch Av	26 B1	Heather Dri	26 B6
Bishops Clo	26 B4	Hermes Clo	26 D2
Bowenhurst Gdns	26 B6	Heron Clo	26 D5
Bowenhurst Rd	26 B6	High Down	26 B1
Bramshot Dri	26 C1	Holland Gdns	26 B3
		Honister Gdns	26 D1
		Hoves Gdns	26 A4
		Howard Clo	26 D2
		Jean Orr Ct	26 B6

Johnsons Way	26 B5	Tudor Way	26 B5
Keats Gdns	26 C2	Upper St	26 A2
Kenilworth Cres	26 D1	Velmead Clo	26 C4
Kenilworth Rd	26 C2	Velmead Rd	26 B4
Kenmore Clo	26 C6	Victoria Ct	26 B2
Kent Rd	26 C2	Victoria Rd	26 A2
Kevins Gro	26 D5	Victoria Hill Rd	26 A1
Kingfisher Clo	26 C6	Vivian Clo	26 C5
Kings Keep	26 B5	Walton Clo	26 A3
Kings Rd	26 B1	Warren Clo	26 C4
Kingscroft	26 B1	Waverley Av	26 B1
Knoll Clo	26 B1	Weldon Clo	26 C6
Knoll Rd	26 B1	Wellington Av	26 C1
*Laburnum Gdns,		Westminster Clo	26 B1
Azalea Gdns	26 C6	Westover Rd	26 C2
Larchfield Rd	26 C4	Whinholt	26 B4
Lawrence Rd	26 A3	Wickham Clo	26 A5
Leawood Rd	26 A3	Wickham Pl	26 A5
Lennel Gdns	26 D5	Wickham Rd	26 A5
Lestock Way	26 D2	Williams Way	26 D2
Lingmala Gro	26 C6	Winchcombe Clo	26 B3
Linkway	26 B5	Wood La	26 D2
Lion Way	26 A2	Woodlands	26 A1
Lismoyne Clo	26 A1	Woodleigh	26 B3
Little Copse	26 B4	Woodside Gdns	26 D1
Long Down	26 A5	Wynne Gdns	26 C6
Longmead	26 B5		
Lyndford Ter	26 B4		
Madeley Rd	26 C5		
Magnolia Way	26 A6		
Medonte Clo	26 C3		

FORDINGBRIDGE

Montrose Clo	26 C3	Albion Rd	27 F2
Moore Clo	26 C6	Alexandra Rd	27 E2
Moore Rd	26 B4	Allenwater Dri	27 D2
Moorlands Clo	26 C3	Ashford Clo	27 C3
New Rd	26 C5	Ashford Rd	27 B4
Newlands	26 B5	Avon Meade	27 D1
Norris Hill Rd	26 D3	Bartons Rd	27 E3
Northfield Clo	26 D5	Beacon Ct	27 E1
Northfield Rd	26 D5	Bedford Clo	27 E1
Oakley Dri	26 C3	Beechwood	27 C3
Old School Clo	26 B3	Bowerwood Rd	27 B4
Osborne Dri	26 C4	Bridge St	27 F3
Park Hill	26 B6	Brook Ter	27 E4
Park Pl	26 B6	Bruyn Ct	27 F2
Parsons Clo	26 A4	Bruyn Rd	27 F2
Peatmoor Clo	26 A1	Brympton Clo	27 B2
Pine Gro	26 C5	Burgate Fields	27 F1
Pines Rd	26 A1	Burnham Rd	27 E1
Pinwood Hill	26 B3	Bushells Farm	27 E4
Pondtail Clo	26 D3	Charnwood Dri	27 E1
Pondtail Gdns	26 D3	Church Farm	27 E4
Pondtail Rd	26 B6	Church St	27 E4
Portland Dri	26 C3	Cottage Mews	27 D2
Priors Keep	26 C3	Diamond Clo	27 E4
Queen Mary Clo	26 A1	Diamond Ct	27 E4
Queens Rd	26 C4	Down Wood Clo	27 C2
Reading Rd Nth	26 A2	Dudley Av	27 E1
Reading Rd Sth	26 A3	Elmwood Av	27 B2
Regent Clo	26 C3	Flaxfields End	27 D3
Regent St	26 B4	Fordingbridge By Pass	27 F4
Richmond Clo	26 B5	Garendon Ct	27 E1
Ridley Clo	26 A4	Green La	27 E2
Rochester Gro	26 B3	Hertford Clo	27 E1
Rose Walk	26 B1	High St	27 E3
Rosedene Gdns	26 A1	Jubilee Ct	27 B3
Rounton Rd	26 C5	Jubilee Rd	27 B3
Rowan Clo	26 D2	Langley Gdns	27 F1
Rufford Clo	26 C6	Lower Bartons	27 E3
Rushmoor Clo	26 C4	Lyster Rd	27 F2
Russetts Dri	26 B3	Manor Ct	27 F3
Rydal Dri	26 A6	Manor Farm Rd	27 A2
Ryebeck Rd	26 B6	Marbean Clo	27 B2
Ryelaw Rd	26 B6	Market Pl	27 E3
St James Rd	26 B3	Marl La	27 B1
St Michaels Clo	26 E3	Mayfield Rd	27 A2
St Philips Ct	26 C5	Mayfly Clo	27 E1
Sian Clo	26 C5	Meadow Av	27 E2
Shelley Clo	26 B3	Meadow Clo	27 E2
Silver Birch Clo	26 A6	Meadow Ct	27 E2
Silver Dale	26 B5	Merton Clo	27 E1
Silver Park Clo	26 C5	Mill Ct	27 E3
Southby Dri	26 C2	Moxhams	27 E3
Spencer Clo	26 D5	Mulberry Gdns	27 E4
Spring Woods	26 A4	Nomandy Way	27 D2
Springfield La	26 A2	Oaklands Clo	27 D2
Stanton Dri	26 A3	Orchard Clo	27 F2
Stockton Av	26 A2	Orchard Gdns	27 E4
Streamside	26 B3	Padstow Pl	27 D4
Sunnyside	26 A1	Park Rd	27 F2
Sycamore Cres	26 A5	Parsonage Clo	27 E3
Tavistock Rd	26 A2	Parsonage Park Dri	27 D2
The Aloes	26 C3	Pealsham Gdns	27 D2
The Avenue	26 A5	Pembridge Rd	27 F1
The Bourne	26 B1	Pennys Clo	27 E1
The Cedars	26 B2	Pennys Cres	27 F1
The Laurels	26 D1	Pennys La	27 E1
The Mount	26 A4	Picket Clo	27 E2
The Verne	26 D2	Player Ct	27 F1
Thirlmere Cres	26 A6	Provost St	27 E4

Puddleslosh La	27 C1		
Queens Gdns	27 F2		
Riverdale Clo	27 F2		
Roman Quay	27 F3		
Round Hill	27 F3		
St Georges Cres	27 E1		
St Georges Rd	27 E1		
Salisbury Rd	27 F3		
Salisbury St	27 F3		
Sandle Copse	27 A2		
Sandleheath Rd	27 A2		
Shaftesbury St	27 E3		
Sharpley Clo	27 E1		
Station Rd	27 C3		
Stephen Martin Gdns	27 D2		
The Bartons	27 E3		
The Pantiles	27 C3		
The Old Vineries	27 B3		
*The Quadrant,			
Brook Ter	27 E4		
Victoria Gdns	27 C3		
Victoria Rd	27 C3		
Vimoutiers Ct	27 D3		
Waverley Ct	27 E1		
Waverley Rd	27 E1		
West St	27 E3		
Whitsbury Rd	27 E1		
Willow Av	27 E2		

GOSPORT

Albert St	28 A3
Astra Walk	28 B4
Avenue Rd	28 A3
Battenburg Rd	28 A3
Bemisters La	28 C4
Bevis Rd	28 A3
Blake Rd	28 A3
Burnhams Walk	28 C4
Carlton Rd	28 A4
Carlton Way	28 B3
Church Pth	28 C4
Clarence Rd	28 B3
Cranbourne Rd	28 A5
Creek Rd	28 B4
Crossland Clo	28 A6
Dock Rd	28 A5
Dolman Rd	28 B5
Dolphin Cres	28 A6
Elizabeth Pl	28 A3
Elmhurst Rd	28 A4
Endeavour Clo	28 B4
Esplanade	28 D4
Farriers Walk	28 B3
Ferrol Rd	28 A2
Forton Rd	28 A3
Fry Rd	28 A3
George St	28 A3
Grove Av	28 A3
Grove Bldgs	28 A4
Harbour Rd	28 C3
Harbour Tower	28 C4
Haslar Bri	28 C5
Haslar Rd	28 C5
Henry St	28 B4
High St	28 C4
Hilton Rd	28 A5
Hobbs Pass	28 C4
Holly St	28 A4
Hornet Clo	28 A4
Jamaica Pl	28 A4
Joseph St	28 A4
Kensington Rd	28 A5
King St	28 B3
Kings Rd	28 A3
Leonard Rd	28 A3
Leventhorpe Pl	28 A4
Leyland Clo	28 A5
Mariners Way	28 B5
Mayfield Rd	28 A5
Molesworth Rd	28 A5
Mumby Rd	28 B3
North Cross St	28 C4
North St	28 C4
Nyria Way	28 B4
Oak St	28 A4
Old Rd	28 A5
Ordnance Rd	28 B4
Parham Rd	28 A2
Pearce Ct	28 A3
Peel Rd	28 A3
Percy Rd	28 A5
Prince of Wales Rd	28 B4
Queens Rd	28 A3
Rampart Row	28 C5
Sea Horse Walk	28 C5
Seaward Tower	28 C5
Shaftesbury Rd	28 A5

Shamrock Clo	28 B4
South Cross St	28 C4
South St	28 A5
Spring Garden La	28 B4
Stoke Gdns	28 A4
Stoke Rd	28 A4
Strathmore Rd	28 A4
Sunbeam Way	28 A6
Sydney Rd	28 A4
Tamworth Rd	28 A5
The Anchorage	28 A5
The Mews	28 C4
The Precinct	28 C4
Thornbrake Rd	28 A5
Thorngate Way	28 C4
Trinity Clo	28 C4
Trinity Grn	28 C4
Victoria St	28 A3
Walpole Rd	28 B4
Weevil La	28 B2
White Lion Walk	28 C3
Willis Rd	28 B4
Wises All	28 C4
Woodley Rd	28 A5
Woodstock Rd	28 A5

HAVANT

Abbotstone Av	29 C1
Adhurst Rd	29 C1
Adsdean Clo	29 A1
Alresford Rd	29 A1
Anderson Clo	29 C2
Barncroft Way	29 A2
Bartons Rd	29 D1
Battens Way	29 B1
Bedford Clo	29 D5
Bedhampton Way	29 B1
Beechworth Rd	29 B4
Bellair Rd	29 C4
Berkeley Sq	29 D4
Bladon Clo	29 D2
Blackdown Cres	29 A1
Blendworth Cres	29 A2
Blenheim Gdns	29 D3
Botley Dri	29 A1
Boundary Way	29 A4
Braishfield Rd	29 C1
Brambles Clo	29 D2
Brockhampton La	29 A4
Brockhampton Rd	29 A4
Brocklands	29 A4
Brookfield Clo	29 A3
Brookmead Way	29 B5
Brookside Rd	29 A5
Burrows Clo	29 C2
Carisbrooke Clo	29 D3
Castle Av	29 D4
Castle Way	29 D4
Catherington Way	29 B1
Chidham Clo	29 A3
Chidham Dri	29 A3
Chidham Sq	29 A3
Chilcombe Clo	29 B2
Church La	29 D5
Civic Centre Rd	29 B3
Clarendon Rd	29 A4
Colemore Sq	29 B1
Compton Clo	29 B2
Connaught Rd	29 C4
Corhampton Cres	29 A1
Cross Way	29 A3
Crossland Dri	29 B2
Denvilles Clo	29 D3
Ditcham Cres	29 A1
Douglas Gdns	29 C1
Downley Rd	29 D2
Dunhurst Clo	29 D2
Dunsbury Way	29 A1
East St	29 B4
Eastern Rd	29 B3
Elder Rd	29 D2
Ellisfield Rd	29 A1
Elm La	29 B4
Elm Park Rd	29 B3
Elm Rd	29 C5
Elmleigh Rd	29 B3
Emsworth Rd	29 C4
Eversley Cres	29 A1
Faber Clo	29 C1
Fair Oak Dri	29 B2
Fairfield Rd	29 B4
Farringdon Rd	29 C1
Fifth Av	29 D3
First Av	29 D3
Fitzwygram Cres	29 A2
Flexford Gdns	29 C2
Fourth Av	29 D3

Fraser Rd	29 A3
Gaulter Clo	29 C2
Glenleigh Park	29 D3
Grange Clo	29 D3
Granville Clo	29 C4
Grove Rd	29 B4
Hallett Rd	29 D3
Hamilton Clo	29 B5
Harestock Rd	29 A2
Hermitage Clo	29 A1
Highclere Av	29 A1
Hipley Rd	29 C2
Hodges Clo	29 C2
Holybourne Rd	29 B2
Homewell	29 B4
Hornbeam Rd	29 D2
Horsebridge Rd	29 C1
INDUSTRIAL ESTATES:	
The Tanneries Ind Est	29 A4
James Rd	29 A3
Juniper Sq	29 B5
Kingsworth Rd	29 B5
Langbrook Clo	29 B6
Langstone Av	29 B6
Langstone Rd	29 B5
Lavant Dri	29 C2
Leigh Rd	29 B3
Liam Clo	29 C1
Linden Way	29 B2
Littlegreen Av	29 C2
Littleton Gro	29 B1
Lockerley Rd	29 C2
Longmead Gdns	29 B6
Lower Grove Rd	29 C5
Luard Ct	29 D4
Lymbourn Rd	29 C4
Manor Clo	29 B4
Market Par	29 B4
Marlborough Park	29 D2
Martin Rd	29 C1
Mavis Cres	29 B3
Meadowlands	29 C4
Medstead Rd	29 B2
Mill La	29 B6
Monterey Dri	29 C1
Montgomery Rd	29 C4
Muccleshell Clo	29 C1
Netherfield Clo	29 C4
New La	29 C3
New Rd	29 A3
Nicholson Way	29 A2
Nightingale Park	29 D4
Norris Gdns	29 C5
North Clo	29 C5
North St	29 B4
North Way	29 A4
Nutwick Rd	29 D2
Oak Park Dri	29 C2
Oaklands Rd	29 C2
Old Copse Rd	29 C2
Orchard Rd	29 B5
Park Par	29 B1
Park Rd North	29 B3
Park Rd South	29 B4
Park Way	29 A4
Pembury Rd	29 C5
Petersfield Rd	29 B3
Pine Gro	29 C4
Pook La	29 C6
Prince Georges St	29 B4
Purbrook Way	29 A1
Rectory Rd	29 B5
Red Lynch Clo	29 D1
Redwood Gro	29 C5
Regents Ct	29 B5
Riders Green	29 A1
Riders La	29 A1
River Way	29 G2
Rowan Rd	29 D2
Russell Rd	29 B2
Rycroft	29 D4
St Albans Rd	29 C1
St Francis Pl	29 A2
St Georges Av	29 A4
School Rd	29 A4
Second Av	29 D3
Selbourne Rd	29 A4
Shawfield Rd	29 C5
Slindon Gdns	29 B5
Soberton Rd	29 A2
Solent Rd	29 A4
South Clo	29 C5
South St	29 B4
Southbrook Clo	29 B5
Southbrook Rd	29 B5
Southleigh Rd	29 D4
Stanbridge Rd	29 D2
Staunton Rd	29 A3

Stockheath La	29 A3
Stockheath Rd	29 A1
Stockheath Way	29 B2
Stone Sq	29 B1
Stroudwood Rd	29 B2
Sunnyheath	29 A1
Swallows Clo	29 D3
Swarraton Rd	29 C2
Tavistock Gdns	29 D4
The Drive	29 B2
The Forum	29 A3
The Gardens	29 D5
The Limes	29 B5
The Mallards	29 B6
The Mews	29 A1
The Pallant	29 B4
The Parchment	29 B4
Third Av	29 C3
Tidworth Rd	29 B1
Timsbury Cres	29 A3
Town Hall Rd	29 B4
Trosnant Rd	29 A3
Union Rd	29 A4
Wade Court Rd	29 C5
Wade La	29 C5
Warblington Av	29 D4
Waterloo Rd	29 B3
Wendover Rd	29 A3
West St	29 A4
West St Arcade	29 B4
Western Rd	29 A3
Whiteladies Clo	29 C4
Willow Clo	29 C4
Wilverley Av	29 C1
Winkton Clo	29 A2
Woodbury Av	29 B5
Woodgreen Av	29 A2
Woodlands Way	29 B1
Woodpecker Clo	29 D4

HEATH END/ TADLEY

Abbots Wood	30 D4
Adam Clo	30 B2
Almswood Rd	30 C1
Ambrose Rd	30 D2
Appleshaw Clo	30 D3
Arnwood Av	30 F2
Ash La	30 A2
Ashurst Clo	30 D3
Barlows Rd	30 D3
Baughurst Rd	30 A2
Beavers Clo	30 C2
Binley Ct	30 E3
Birch Rd	30 B1
Bishops Clo	30 D2
Bishopswood La	30 A2
Bishopswood Rd	30 C2
Blakes La	30 E2
Bordon Clo	30 D3
Bowmonts Rd	30 F3
Bracken Wood	30 D2
Brackenwood Dri	30 D2
Bramdean Clo	30 D3
Brampton Meadow	30 F3
Briar Way	30 E3
Brimpton Rd	30 A2
Broadhalfpenny La	30 E2
Brook Green	30 F3
Brookside Walk	30 F3
Burnham Rd	30 C1
Burnley Clo	30 D3
Candover Clo	30 E3
*Carrington Cres,	
Mount Pleasant	30 D3
Cedar Clo	30 F4
Cheriton Clo	30 D3
Chippendale Clo	30 B1
Christy Ct	30 E3
Church Brook	30 C4
Church Rd	30 D4
Churchill Clo	30 F4
Conifer Clo	30 A1
Coppice Clo	30 A2
Crookham Clo	30 D4
Deanswood Rd	30 C2
Denmead	30 D3
Douro Clo	30 A2
Droxford Cres	30 D3
Elmhurst	30 E3
Fairlawn Rd	30 F4
Fairoak Way	30 A1
Falcon Fields	30 D1
Farrington Way	30 D4
Finch Clo	30 E4
Fir Tree Cnr	30 A1
Forest Clo	30 A1

Forest La	30 F4
Franklin Av	30 C1
Fullerton Way	30 E3
Furze Rd	30 C1
Giles Ct	30 F3
Giles Rd	30 F3
Glebe Clo	30 F4
Glendale Rd	30 D2
Gorselands	30 E2
Graveley Clo	30 E4
Greywell Clo	30 D3
Guttridge La	30 D4
Hamble Dri	30 F3
Hangar Rd	30 C1
Harmsworth Rd	30 E3
Hartley Gdns	30 E4
Hartshill Rd	30 B2
Hawkley Dri	30 D4
Hazel Grn	30 A2
Heath Ct	30 B1
Heath End Rd	30 A2
Heather Dri	30 C1
Heathlands	30 A2
Heathrow Copse	30 A2
Hedge End	30 E4
Hepplewhite Clo	30 B1
Herriard Way	30 E4
Hillcrest	30 E2
Hinton Clo	30 D3
Honeybottom Rd	30 D2
Huntsmoor Rd	30 B2
Hylton Ct	30 F3
Hythe Clo	30 D3
INDUSTRIAL ESTATES:	
Bartley Wood Business	
Park (West)	30 E4
Inhurst Way	30 B2
Lake Ct	30 F3
Lamdens Walk	30 E4
Linton Clo	30 F4
Litchfield Ho	30 D2
Long Gro	30 A1
Malthouse La	30 E3
Maple Gro	30 D2
Meon Clo	30 D2
Millers Rd	30 D3
Minstead Clo	30 E4
Monkswood Cres	30 D4
Mornington Clo	30 A2
Mortimer Gdns	30 E4
Mount Pleasant	30 D3
Mount Pleasant Dri	30 D2
Mulfords Hill	30 D1
New Rd	30 D4
Newchurch Rd	30 C2
Newtown	30 D2
Northview Rd	30 F4
Oak Clo	30 A2
Oaktree Clo	30 D2
Odette Gdns	30 E2
Otterbourne Clo	30 E4
Peters Clo	30 D4
Pinehurst	30 D4
Pinewood Clo	30 A1
Pinks La	30 B1
Plantation Rd	30 B1
Pleasant Hill	30 D3
Poplar Clo	30 A2
Portway	30 A1
Priors Rd	30 C1
Purbrook Rd	30 D3
Ramsdell Clo	30 D4
Rectory Clo	30 E4
Reynards Clo	30 D3
Rimes La	30 B4
Ropley Clo	30 D3
Rosebank Clo	30 E3
Rotherwick Rd	30 E4
Rowan Clo	30 F3
Rowan Rd	30 F3
Sandford Rd	30 C2
Sandy La	30 F3
Sarisbury Clo	30 D3
Sarum Rd	30 C1
Selborne Walk	30 D3
Shaw La	30 B4
Sheridan Cres	30 B2
Shyshack La	30 B1
Silchester Rd	30 E2
Silverdale Rd	30 D2
Smallwood Dri	30 D2
Southdown Rd	30 D2
Spiers Clo	30 F3
Stanfield	30 D2
Stephens Rd	30 E3
Stoke House	30 D2
Stratfield Av	30 E4
Stratfield Ct	30 E3
Swains Clo	30 E3
Swains Rd	30 E3

Swanwick Walk	30 D3
Swedish Houses	30 F4
Sympson Rd	30 F2
Tadley Common Rd	30 E3
Tadley Hill	30 E3
The Green	30 E4
The Hawthorns	30 A2
The Lane	30 A2
The Oaks	30 D3
The Old Forge	30 A2
The Orchard	30 F3
The Warren	30 D3
*Titchfield Clo,	
Herriard Way	30 E4
Tomlins Clo	30 D4
Tudor Ct	30 D2
Tunworth Mews	30 F3
Vinetree Clo	30 F4
Warbington Clo	30 E4
Wellington Cres	30 A2
West St	30 F3
Westfield Clo	30 F3
Weyhill Clo	30 D4
Whitedown Rd	30 C2
Wickham Clo	30 E2
Wigmore Rd	30 B2
Wildwood Dri	30 A2
Willow Cnr	30 A1
Willow Rd	30 D3
Winchfield Gdns	30 E4
Winkworth La	30 E1
Winston Av	30 F4
Wolverton Rd	30 A2
Woodcott Ho	30 D2
Woodlands Rd	30 A1

HOOK

Alderwood Dri	31 D1
Appletree Mead	31 F2
Ashlea	31 D1
Aspen Gdns	31 E1
Bandhall Pl	31 D3
Bartley Way	31 E4
Beechcrest Vw	31 D1
Bell Meadow Rd	31 D3
Berry Ct	31 D4
Birch Gro	31 D1
Bluehaven Walk	31 A3
Bowfield	31 F2
Bowling Green Dri	31 A3
Bramshott Dri	31 D3
Broad Leaze	31 C1
Brown Croft	31 B3
Butts Meadow	31 B3
Carlton Clo	31 B3
Chalkey Copse	31 C1
Charles Clo	31 C2
Cherry Clo	31 D1
Church Path	31 A3
Church Vw	31 D3
Coltsfoot Pl	31 F2
Compass Field	31 E3
Compton Clo	31 D3
Dorchester Rd	31 C3
Driftway Rd	31 F3
Elms Rd	31 C2
Farm Ground Clo	31 F2
Ferndale Gdns	31 C2
Ferrell Field	31 A3
Four Acre Coppice	31 E2
Frouds Clo	31 B3
Garden Clo	31 B2
Goose Grn	31 B2
Goose La	31 C2
Gower Cres	31 D3
Grand Parade	31 C3
Great Shaldons	
Coppice	31 B2
Griffin Way Nth	31 D1
Griffin Way Sth	31 E2
Harfield Clo	31 C2
Hawthorne Rise	31 D1
Hazel Coppice	31 D1
Heath View	31 F2
Holt Way	31 F2
Hopgarden Rd	31 A3
Hornbeam Pl	31 D1
Hunts Clo	31 E3
INDUSTRIAL ESTATES:	
Bartley Wood	
Business Pk West	31 E4
Meridian Business Pk	31 D4
Osborne Way Ind Est	31 D4
John Morgan Clo	31 C1
Kerfield Way	31 D3
Lay Field	31 B3
Lees Meadow	31 F2
Little Sheldons	31 B2

61

London Rd	31 A4
Lynwood Gdns	31 C2
Mead Hatchgate	31 C1
Memorial Rd	31 B4
Middle Mead	31 B2
New Rd	31 C3
Newnham Park	31 A4
Newnham Rd	31 A4
Nightingale Gdns	31 C2
Nursery Clo	31 B1
Oakhanger Clo	31 D3
Oak Tree Dri	31 D1
Osborn Way	31 D4
Painters Pightle	31 A2
Pantile Dri	31 F2
Quince Tree Way	31 E3
Raven Rd	31 C3
Ravenscroft	31 E2
Rawlings Rd	31 D4
Reading Rd	31 C1
Rectory Rd	31 C4
Rookswood	31 D2
Rosebay Gdns	31 F2
St Johns Clo	31 D3
Scots Ct	31 F1
Scures Rd	31 B3
Searles La	31 F1
Seton Dri	31 A4
Shaw Pightle	31 B2
Selborne Clo	31 E3
Sheldons La	31 B3
Sheldons Rd	31 C3
Small Field Dri	31 F1
Squarefield Gdns	31 E2
Stable Clo	31 B3
Station Rd	31 D4
The Orchard	31 C1
The Spinney	31 C2
Trust Clo	31 B3
Valmead Clo	31 D3
Vetch Field	31 E3
Wagon La	31 D2
Wash Brook	31 C1
Wheelers Hill	31 E3
Whites Clo	31 A3
Whitewater Rise	31 F2
Wild Herons	31 F3

HYTHE

Abbey Clo	32 C3
Adams Way	32 C3
Admirals Way	32 B1
Alexandra Clo	32 B2
Alexandra Rd	32 B2
Amberslade Walk	32 B5
Andrew Clo	32 C5
Armada Dri	32 B4
Armitage Av	32 B5
Arnwood Av	32 C6
Ash Clo	32 D6
Ashford Cres	32 C2
Ashley Clo	32 D5
Astra Ct	32 A1
Atheling Rd	32 B2
Badgers Walk	32 B4
Barclay Mews	32 C5
Beaulieu Rd	32 B4
Beech Cres	32 D6
Belmont Clo	32 C4
Belvedere Rd	32 C4
Beverley Rd	32 B6
Birchdale	32 D4
Blackdown Clo	32 A5
Blenheim Clo	32 A5
Blenheim Mws	32 C5
Boundstone	32 A4
Braehead	32 B4
Bramble Ct	32 B4
Brecon Clo	32 A4
Briar Ct	32 B4
Brinton La	32 B1
Bullrush Clo	32 B5
Buttercup Clo	32 C4
Butts Bridge Hill	32 C6
Buttsash Av	32 C6
Buttsash Gdns	32 C5
Buttsash Rd	32 C6
Byeways	32 B4
Carpenter Clo	32 B2
Cedar Rd	32 D6
Challenger Way	32 A4
Chaloner Cres	32 C5
Chaveney Clo	32 B5
Coat Gdns	32 B2
Conifer Clo	32 A3
Copse Clo	32 B5
Copsewood Rd	32 A3
Corbold Rd	32 B6
Cormorant Dri	32 D3
Crete Cotts	32 B5
Crete La	32 B5
Curlew Clo	32 D3
Curlew Dri	32 D3
Dale Rd	32 A3
Deerleap Clo	32 C3
Deerleap Way	32 C3
Devonshire Gdns	32 C3
Dibden Lodge Clo	32 A2
Douglas Way	32 A2
Drakes Clo	32 B4
Drummond Rd	32 B2
Dukeswood Dri	32 C4
Edward Rd	32 B2
Elgin Clo	32 C3
Elizabeth Gdns	32 C5
Elm Cres	32 D6
Endeavour Way	32 A1
Ewart Ct	32 B2
Fair View Clo	32 B3
Fair View Dri	32 B3
Fairfield Clo	32 B3
Fairview Parade	32 B4
Fairway Rd	32 A3
Fawley Rd	32 D5
Fern Rd	32 A3
Fernhills Rd	32 C4
Ferry Rd	32 B3
Fleuret Clo	32 D5
Forest Front	32 C6
Forest Hill Way	32 B4
Forest Meadow	32 C6
Foxbury Clo	32 C4
Foxtail Dri	32 B5
Frays Lea	32 C4
Frog Hall La	32 C4
Frost La	32 C5
Fulmer Dri	32 D3
Furzedale Gdns	32 D4
Furzedale Pk	32 D4
Furzedown Mews	32 D4
Furzey Av	32 C3
Gannet Clo	32 D3
Glenside	32 B3
Golden Hind Pk	32 B4
Grays Av	32 C2
Greatwood Clo	32 C4
Green Clo	32 B2
Greenacre	32 B5
Grenville Gdns	32 C5
Guillemot Clo	32 D4
Hamilton Mews	32 D4
Hamilton Rd	32 D4
Hardley La	32 D6
Hardy Dri	32 D3
Hart Hill	32 D3
Hartley Clo	32 C5
Harvey Gdns	32 C2
Hawthorn Rd	32 A3
Hayley Clo	32 C5
Haynes Way	32 A5
Heatherstone Av	32 B6
Heathfield	32 B4
High St	32 B1
Highlands Clo	32 B4
Highlands Way	32 B4
Hillview Rd	32 A3
Hirst Clo	32 C3
Hobart Dri	32 C2
Holly Clo	32 D6
Hollybank Clo	32 B3
Hollybank Cres	32 A2
Hollybank Rd	32 A3
Home Farm Clo	32 B3
Hotspur Clo	32 A2
Hythe By-Pass	32 A6

INDUSTRIAL ESTATES:

The Shipyard Industrial	32 C1
Ingle Glen	32 C4
Ipley Way	32 C4
Jessop Clo	32 A1
Jessop Walk	32 A1
Jones La	32 A2
Kelvin Clo	32 B3
Kiln Clo	32 A4
Knightstone Grange	32 C3
Knightwood Rd	32 C3
Laburnam Cres	32 D6
Ladycross Rd	32 C4
Lambourne Clo	32 B5
Lammas Rd	32 C4
Lanehays Rd	32 B3
Langdown Lawn	32 C3
Langdown Lawn Clo	32 B4
Langdown Rd	32 C2
Laurel Clo	32 A3
Lime Walk	32 A5
Lodge Rd	32 C5
Longmeadow Gdns	32 B2
Lower Mullins La	32 A3
Lunedale Rd	32 B6
Lynwood Clo	32 C4
Lytton Rd	32 C3
Malwood Rd	32 A2
Malwood Rd W	32 A3
Mansell Clo	32 A6
Maple Rd	32 D5
Marlborough Ct	32 A4
Mendip Gdns	32 A5
Merrie Mead Clo	32 B6
Merrivale Clo	32 A3
Michael Way	32 A2
Midway	32 B4
Millers Way	32 B4
Monks Walk	32 B6
Mount House Clo	32 A1
Mountfield	32 A2
Mousehole La	32 B2
Nash Clo	32 A5
Nash Rd	32 A5
Nelson Ct	32 D4
New Rd	32 B2
Noads Clo	32 B4
Noads Way	32 B5
North Rd	32 A5
Northbourne Clo	32 C5
Oak Clo	32 A6
Oak Rd	32 A6
Orchard Way	32 A4
Overbrook	32 B4
Park Clo	32 C2
Partridge Rd	32 C5
Pear Tree Rd	32 A4
Percy Clo	32 A1
Pine Clo	32 B4
Pinewood Dri	32 D4
Prospect Pl	32 B1
Pylewell Rd	32 B1
Queens Clo	32 C3
Racketts	32 B3
Ranfurly Gdns	32 B5
Ratcliffe Rd	32 A2
Roberts Rd	32 A2
Roman Gdns	32 A6
Roman Rd	32 A6
Roman Way	32 A6
Rose Clo	32 C4
Roseberry Av	32 C3
Saddlers La	32 C4
St Johns St	32 B1
Sandilands Way	32 B2
School Rd	32 B2
Seaward Rd	32 C2
Shamrock Way	32 B1
Shoblands Way	32 C4
Shore Rd	32 C2
Silver End	32 C4
Solent Dri	32 A3
Solent Rd	32 B6
South St	32 B2
Southampton Rd	32 A2
Spinney Dale	32 D3
Spinney Gdns	32 D4
Spring Clo	32 B2
Squirrels Walk	32 D6
Stokesay Clo	32 B4
Sunningdale	32 A3
Sycamore Rd	32 A6
Talbot Rd	32 D6
Tamar Gro	32 A3
Tates Rd	32 A5
Tern Clo	32 D3
The Marsh	32 A4
The Mead	32 A4
The Promenade	32 B1
The Vale	32 B4
The Wicket	32 B4
Tormead	32 A4
Trafalgar Way	32 D4
Upper Mullins La	32 A4
Valley Dene	32 B4
Velsheda Ct	32 B1
Villers Rd	32 B6
Warrys Clo	32 C5
Water La	32 A5
Watermans La	32 B5
Waterside	32 A1
Wellington Clo	32 A6
West Hill Dri	32 A2
West Rd	32 A2
West St	32 A2
Westcliffe Walk	32 A3
Whinfield Rd	32 B6
Whitewater Rise	32 B3
Whittington Clo	32 B3
Widecombe Dri	32 A3
Wildground La	32 C5
Windmill Copse	32 B5
Windrush Way	32 C3
Woodlands Clo	32 B5
Woodlands Ct	32 B5
Yelverton Av	32 C5

KINGSCLERE

Anchor Rd	33 C3
Ash Gro	33 D2
Basingstoke Rd	33 D2
Bear Hill	33 B3
Brimley Hill Ct	33 C3
Brimpton Rd	33 D2
Bushnells Dri	33 B2
Byfields Rd	33 C2
Canons Ct	33 B2
Cedar Dri	33 B2
Coppice Rd	33 D2
Cottington Clo	33 D3
Ecchinswell Rd	33 A2
Elm Gro	33 D2
Elm Grove Farm	33 D2
Elm Grove Flats	33 D2
Fawconer Rd	33 D2
Felden Ct	33 C3
Field Gate La	33 B2
Foxs La	33 B3
Frogs Hole	33 B2
Garden Clo	33 D3
Garrett Clo	33 B2
George St	33 C2
Greenacre	33 D2
Greenlands Rd	33 D2
Hardys Field	33 B1
Highams Clo	33 D2
Hollowshot La	33 B4
Hook Rd	33 E3

INDUSTRIAL ESTATES:

Kingsclere Park Ind Est	33 B1
Keeps Mead	33 B1
Kevin Clo	33 F3
King John Rd	33 D3
Kingsclere By-Pass	33 C1
Knowle Cres	33 D3
Larch Dri	33 C3
Link Rd	33 E2
Longcroft Rd	33 B1
Love La	33 D2
Newbury Rd	33 B1
North St	33 C2
Peel Gdns	33 B1
Pennys Hatch	33 E2
Phoenix Ct	33 C2
Popes Hill	33 B2
Poveys Mead	33 E3
Priors Clo	33 D2
Queens Rd	33 E3
Rose Hodson Ct	33 B1
St Marys Rd	33 C3
Sandford Clo	33 F3
South Rd	33 E2
Strokins Rd	33 D2
Sunnyside	33 B3
Swan St	33 B3
The Dell	33 D2
The Lines	33 C1
The Paddock	33 B2
Thorneley Rd	33 D2
Tower Hill	33 B2
Tower Hill Ct	33 B2
Union La	33 C1
Wellmans Meadow	33 B1
Winchester Rd	33 B4
Yew Clo	33 E3

LEE-ON-THE SOLENT

Ajax Clo	34 A1
Anglesea Rd	34 D6
Ashton Way	34 A2
Avon Clo	34 C5
Beach Rd	34 C5
Beverley Rd	34 A2
Blackbird Way	34 C3
Britten Rd	34 B4
Broom Way	34 C3
Brune La	34 D1
Bullfinch Ct	34 C3
Cambridge Rd	34 C5
Chaffinch La	34 C3
Chark La	34 C3
Cheltenham Cres	34 C4
Cherque La	34 D3
Cherry Clo	34 D5
Cheyne Way	34 D5
Chilcomb Clo	34 D5
Clanwilliam Rd	34 C5
Clifton Rd	34 D6
Common Barn La	34 C3
Compton Clo	34 D5
Conqueror Way	34 A1
Cornfield Rd	34 C4
Court Barn Clo	34 C3
Court Barn La	34 C3
Court Rd	34 B4
Cremyll Clo	34 A1
Crofton Av	34 A3
Cross Rd	34 D6
Dallington Clo	34 A2
Deane Gdns	34 D4
Deansgate	34 A1
Derwent Rd	34 C5
Drake Rd	34 A3
East Cliff Clo	34 C3
East House Av	34 A1
Elmore Av	34 D5
Elmore Clo	34 D6
Elmore Rd	34 D6
Epsom Walk	34 D4
Esmonde Clo	34 C4
Esplanade	34 B5
Fell Dri	34 C4
Ferncroft Clo	34 A1
Fieldhouse Dri	34 D3
Francis Clo	34 D5
Gibson Clo	34 D4
Glenthorne Clo	34 A2
Goldfinch La	34 C3
Gosport Rd	34 D6
Green Link	34 C5
Grenville Rd	34 B3
Grove Rd	34 C4
Harrier Clo	34 D4
Hawthorn Walk	34 C4
Headley Clo	34 D4
High St	34 C5
Hiller Walk	34 D4
Hollybank	34 C5
Inverkip Clo	34 B3
Jersey Clo	34 A2
Kenilworth Clo	34 C4
Kimpton Clo	34 D4
Kings Rd	34 B4
Kingsmead Av	34 A2
Lakeside	34 C6
Larch Clo	34 D5
Laurus Walk	34 D4
Leamington Cres	34 C4
Leviathan Clo	34 A1
Link Way	34 A2
Lulworth Rd	34 C5
Magpie La	34 C3
Maizemore Walk	34 C4
Manor Way	34 C4
Maple Clo	34 D5
Marine Parade E	34 B5
Marine Parade W	34 A3
Martin Clo	34 C3
Mayflower Clo	34 A1
Milvil Rd	34 B4
Monks Hill	34 A3
Montserrat Rd	34 B4
Moody Rd	34 A1
Mulberry Av	34 A2
Newton Pl	34 B4
Northways	34 B1
Norwich Pl	34 B3
Nottingham Pl	34 B4
Nursery La	34 A1
Olave Clo	34 C4
Orion Clo	34 A1
Osborne Rd	34 B4
Osprey Clo	34 D4
Petrie Rd	34 C4
Pier St	34 B5
Portsmouth Rd	34 C6
Promenade	34 A3
Queens Clo	34 B4
Queens Rd	34 C6
Raynes Rd	34 D6
Richmond Rd	34 B4
Rosemary Walk	34 C4
Ross Way	34 C4
Rowan Clo	34 D5
Rowner Rd	34 D1
Russell Clo	34 C4
Russell Rd	34 C5
Ryde Pl	34 D6
Salisbury Ter	34 C4
Sandhill La	34 D3
Sea Crest Rd	34 D4
Sea La	34 A2

Shore Clo	38 E4	
Shorefield Rd	38 A1	
Shorefield Cres	38 C2	
Shorefield Way	38 C2	
Solent Pines	38 B3	
Solent Way	38 F3	
Studlands Dri	38 C3	
Swallow Dri	38 F3	
Sycamore Clo	38 D2	
The Boltons	38 D4	
The Bucklers	38 B2	
The Green	38 E3	
The Orchard	38 E3	
Victoria Rd	38 C3	
Vinegar Hill	38 D2	
Wayside Clo	38 D2	
West Rd	38 B2	
Westminster Rd	38 B3	
Westover Rd	38 D3	
Whitby Rd	38 B3	
Windmill Clo	38 D3	
Wolsey Way	38 E3	
Wood La	38 D3	
Woodland Way	38 C3	

NEW ALRESFORD

Appledown Clo	39 D6
Arle Clo	39 C3
Arle Gdns	39 C4
Arundel Clo	39 C6
Ashburton Clo	39 B5
Ashburton Rd	39 B5
Beech Rd	39 D5
Benenden Grn	39 C6
Bramble Hill	39 C5
Bridge Rd	39 B5
Broad St	39 D4
Buttermere Gdns	39 C6
Carpenters	39 C5
Carisbrooke Clo	39 C6
Chestnut Walk	39 D5
Chiltern Ct	39 C5
Colden La	39 D2
Coniston Gdns	39 D6
Corfe Clo	39 C6
Covey Way	39 B6
Culley View	39 C5
De-Lucy Av	39 A5
Derwent Gdns	39 C6
Dickenson Walk	39 C6
Dorian Gro	39 B5
Dover Clo	39 C6
Down Gate	39 C6
Drove La	39 A4
East St	39 D4
Ellingham Clo	39 C4
Elm Rd	39 C5
Ennerdale Gdns	39 D6
Fair View	39 C5
Grange Clo	39 B5
Grange Rd	39 B5
Great Weir	39 D3
Green Clo	39 C1
Haig Rd	39 D4
Hasted Dri	39 C6
Hawthorne Clo	39 C5
Headley Clo	39 C6
Jacklyns Clo	39 B6
Jacklyns La	39 B6
Jesty Rd	39 B5
Kiln La	39 D1
Ladywell La	39 C3
Lime Rd	39 C5
Lindley Gdns	39 C6
Linnets Rd	39 C6
Mallard Clo	39 C4
Maple Clo	39 C5
Meadow Clo	39 C5
Meryon Rd	39 B6
Mill Hill	39 C5
Mitford Rd	39 B5
New Alresford By-Pass	39 A6
New Farm Rd	39 A5
Nicholson Pl	39 B5
Nursery Rd	39 C5
Oak Hill	39 C5
Orchard Clo	39 C6
Paddock Way	39 C6
Perins Clo	39 B6
Pound Hill	39 C4
Prospect Rd	39 B6
Robertson Rd	39 B5
Rosebery Rd	39 C5
Russet Clo	39 C5
Salisbury Rd	39 D5
Searles Clo	39 D5
Shepherds Down	39 C6

South Clo	39 B5
South Rd	39 B5
Spring Gdns	39 B6
Spring Way	39 B6
Station App	39 C4
Station Rd	39 D4
Sun Hill Cres	39 D6
Sun La	39 D6
The Avenue	39 A5
The Brook	39 C1
The Dean	39 D2
The George Yard	39 D4
The Soke	39 D3
Tichborne Down	39 B6
Ullswater Gro	39 D6
Watercress Meadow	39 B6
West St	39 C4
Winchester Rd	39 A5
Windermere Gdns	39 C6
Windsor Rd	39 C6
Witton Hill	39 C6

NEW MILTON

Albany Clo	40 B4
Albert Rd	40 B2
Antler Dri	40 A1
Apple Tree Clo	40 C4
Arden Walk	40 D3
Arlington Ct	40 C5
Arnolds Clo	40 B5
Arundel Clo	40 A2
Ashdown Walk	40 D3
Ashley Clo	40 C2
Ashmore Av	40 C5
Aspen Ct	40 C4
Avenue Rd	40 B2
Aysha Clo	40 D3
Baden Clo	40 D3
Ballard Clo	40 C1
Balmoral Walk	40 A2
Barrs Av	40 C1
Barrs Wood Dri	40 C1
Barrs Wood Rd	40 D1
Barton Common La	40 D5
Barton Common Rd	40 C6
Barton Court Av	40 B6
Barton Court Rd	40 B4
Barton Croft	40 B5
Barton Dri	40 B5
Barton Grn	40 C6
Barton La	40 B5
Barton Way	40 B5
Barton Wood Rd	40 A6
Beach Av	40 B6
*Beaulieu Clo, Chatsworth Way	40 A2
Becton La	40 C6
Becton Mead	40 C4
Beechwood Av	40 A1
Bertram Rd	40 D1
Blair Clo	40 A2
Blyths Wood Ct	40 B6
Bouverie Clo	40 B4
Bowland Rise	40 D3
*Braemore Clo, Chatsworth Way	40 A2
Branksome Clo	40 D2
Brook Av	40 C1
Brook Av Nth	40 D1
Brooklyn Ct	40 B2
Brownsea Clo	40 A2
Buckingham Walk	40 A2
Byron Rd	40 A5
Cabot Way	40 B2
Cadhay Clo	40 A2
Caird Av	40 D2
Camella.Gdns	40 C3
Carisbrooke Ct	40 A2
Caslake Clo	40 B4
Cedar Gdns	40 C3
Chaffinch Clo	40 B3
Chatsworth Way	40 A2
Chestnut Av	40 C5
Chiltern Clo	40 B4
Chiltern Dri	40 A4
Christchurch Bay Rd	40 A6
Christchurch Rd	40 A4
Church La	40 B4
Cliff Ter	40 B6
Cliffe Rd	40 A6
Compton Rd	40 B3
Connaught Clo	40 A4
Conway Clo	40 D2
Copse Av	40 D3
Copse Rd	40 D3
Cowper Av	40 C4
Crescent Dri	40 B6

Crest Ct	40 C3
Crossmead Av	40 C3
Culver Rd	40 A3
Danes Clo	40 C6
Daneswood Ct	40 D2
Daneswood Rd	40 D2
Dark La	40 A1
Darren Clo	40 A5
Davis Field	40 A5
Dawkins Way	40 B3
Dilly La	40 C6
Doe Copse Way	40 A1
Dolphin Pl	40 B6
Drake Clo	40 B2
Duart Ct	40 D2
Dunford Clo	40 A4
Durland Clo	40 A3
Eastlands	40 D3
Edmunds Clo	40 B3
Eldon Av	40 A4
Eldon Clo	40 A4
Elm Av	40 C3
Fairfield Rd	40 A1
Farm La	40 B6
Farm La North	40 C5
Fawcett Rd	40 A3
Fawn Gdns	40 B1
Fenleigh Clo	40 C4
Ferndale Rd	40 D1
Fernglade	40 C2
Fernhill La	40 B2
Fernhill Rd	40 B1
Fir Av	40 D3
First Marine Av	40 A5
Foxcote Gdns	40 A2
Franklin Rd	40 D1
Friars Walk	40 B4
Furze Croft	40 B3
Garden Clo	40 C3
Glen Avon	40 D3
Glen Garry	40 D3
Goldfinch Clo	40 B3
Gore Gdns	40 B3
*Gore Grange, Jowitt Dri	40 B3
Gore Rd	40 A3
Green La	40 D5
Greenacre	40 C5
Greenfield Clo	40 C5
Greenwoods	40 D3
Grove Rd	40 B6
Hale Av	40 D3
Hale Gdns	40 D3
Hardy Clo	40 B2
Hart Clo	40 B1
Hatfield Ct	40 A2
Haven Gdns	40 C3
Haysoms Clo	40 C4
Hazelwood Av	40 A1
Heathwood Av	40 A5
Heathy Clo	40 B5
Hedgerley	40 A5
Hengistbury Rd	40 A5
Herbert Rd	40 A2
High Ridge Cres	40 D2
Highbury Clo	40 C5
Highlands Rd	40 C5
Hobart Rd	40 C3
Homewood Clo	40 D2
Howe Clo	40 B2
INDUSTRIAL ESTATES:	
Williams Ind Est	40 A3
Inglegreen Clo	40 A4
Inglewood Dri	40 A3
Janred Ct	40 A6
Jaundrells Clo	40 D2
Jowitt Dri	40 B3
Kenilworth Av	40 D2
Kennard Ct	40 B2
Kennard Rd	40 B1
Keysworth Av	40 B6
Knighton Pl	40 A5
Lake Grove Rd	40 B1
Langdon Clo	40 C4
Larkshill Clo	40 C1
Leigh Rd	40 C1
Linford Clo	40 A4
Linnet Ct	40 B3
Litchford Rd	40 C1
Little Barrs Dri	40 C1
*Longleat Gdns, Chatsworth Way	40 A2
Lymington Rd	40 B4
Lyric Clo	40 A6
Lyon Av	40 B3
Magpie Gro	40 B3
Manor Farm Clo	40 A6
Manor Rd	40 C2
Maple Clo	40 D6

Marine Dri East	40 B6
Marine Dri West	40 A6
Marley Av	40 A1
Marley Clo	40 A2
Marryat Rd	40 B2
Meadow Rd	40 D1
Meadow Way	40 C6
Mendip Clo	40 D3
Milford Rd	40 D4
Milton Gro	40 C3
Milton Mead	40 B3
Mitchell Clo	40 C6
Moat La	40 B4
Moore Clo	40 A4
Moorland Av	40 B4
Mount Av	40 C3
Mount Clo	40 C4
Nelson Clo	40 B2
Newlands Rd	40 C3
Newton Rd	40 D5
Norris Gdns	40 C3
Oak Rd	40 D2
Oakwood Av	40 D1
Old Green Par	40 B4
Old Milton Green	40 B4
Old Milton Rd	40 B4
Orchard Gro	40 C4
Osborne Rd	40 C2
Oxey Clo	40 C4
Palmer Pl	40 C1
Parham Clo	40 A2
Park Rd	40 B4
Parkland Dri	40 A4
Peckham Av	40 B3
Penn Clo	40 B4
Penny Hedge	40 C5
Pilgrims Clo	40 D1
Pine Clo	40 A5
Pleasance Way	40 B2
Pond Clo	40 B2
Powis Clo	40 D2
Prestwood Clo	40 B4
Queensway	40 A2
Raleigh Clo	40 B2
Robin Gro	40 B3
Roebuck Clo	40 D2
Rosewood Gdns	40 A1
Rothbury Pk	40 D3
Royston Pl	40 D5
Rubens Clo	40 C1
Sandmartin Clo	40 B6
Sea Rd	40 A6
Sea Way	40 D5
Seacroft Av	40 A5
Seafield Clo	40 B6
Seafield Rd	40 A5
Seaward Av	40 A6
Second Marine Av	40 C6
Shenstone Ct	40 C4
Silverdale	40 D5
Solent Dri	40 C6
South Av	40 D3
Southern La	40 B5
Southern Oaks	40 B4
Spencer Rd	40 C2
Spinacre	40 C5
Spindlewood Clo	40 B4
Stag Clo	40 A1
Stannington Clo	40 C3
Station Rd	40 C2
Stem La	40 A2
Stirling Clo	40 D2
Stratfield Pl	40 A2
Sunnyfield Rd	40 B5
Tanglewood Ct	40 C2
The Close	40 C5
The Fairway	40 C6
The Hyde	40 A1
The Martells	40 D5
The Vinery	40 D2
The Willows	40 D5
Thoresby Ct	40 A4
Three Acre Clo	40 A4
Three Acre Dri	40 A5
Uplands Av	40 C5
Velvet Lawn Rd	40 A1
Vincent Clo	40 B3
Vincent Rd	40 B2
Violet La	40 C1
Walkford La	40 A2
*Walnut Clo, Kennard Rd	40 B2
Warwick Av	40 D2
Waterford Rd	40 D1
Wavendon Av	40 A5
Waverley Rd	40 C3
Well Clo	40 A3
Wellington St	40 C1
Wendover Clo	40 B3
Wessex Av	40 C3

Westbury Clo	40 C5
White Horses	40 A6
White Knights	40 B6
Whitefield Rd	40 C2
Wick Clo	40 A3
Wick Dri	40 A3
Willowdene Clo	40 D2
Wilton Gdns	40 A2
Winston Ct	40 B4
Wood Vale Gdns	40 D1
Woodlawn Clo	40 B4
Woodlands Rd	40 A6
Worthy Rd	40 B2
Wren Clo	40 B3
York Av	40 C2
York Pl	40 C2

NORTH BADDESLEY

Amberley Clo	41 B2
Ash Clo	41 B2
Baddesley Clo	41 B1
Botley Rd	41 A1
Bracken Clo	41 C3
Bracken Rd	41 C4
Broad La	41 B1
Brook Clo	41 C3
Brownhill Rd	41 C3
Camelia Clo	41 C2
Castle La	41 D2
Cedar Cres	41 B1
Cerne Clo	41 B2
Chilworth Old Village	41 C2
Church Clo	41 C2
Copse Clo	41 B2
Crescent Rd	41 B2
Dibble Dri	41 B3
Dunnings La	41 B1
Edwina Clo	41 C2
Emer Clo	41 C1
Ennel Copse	41 C3
Fielden Clo	41 B3
Firgrove Clo	41 B2
Firgrove Rd	41 B2
Fleming Av	41 C3
Fleming Ct	41 D3
Forest Clo	41 A2
Greenhill Rd	41 A6
Heath Rd	41 C3
Heatherbrae Gdns	41 B3
Highlands Clo	41 A1
Hillcrest Clo	41 B2
Hoe La	41 A3
Hollywood Clo	41 B3
Hulles Way	41 B3
Juniper Clo	41 B1
Laburnum Clo	41 C2
Langham Clo	41 B3
Launcelyn Clo	41 B3
Lavington Gdns	41 B3
Linden Walk	41 B1
Merry Gdns	41 C3
Meadow Clo	41 C3
Middle Rd	41 C2
Mortimer Way	41 B3
Northern Wood Clo	41 B2
Norton Welch Clo	41 D3
Nutburn Rd	41 D2
Orchard Clo	41 B1
Overbrook Way	41 A2
Packridge La	41 A5
Pine Clo	41 B2
Poplar Way	41 B1
Proctor Dri	41 B3
Ringwood Dri	41 A2
Rosslyn Clo	41 C2
Rownhams La	41 B1
Rownhams Rd	41 C3
St Andrews Clo	41 B1
St Christophers Clo	41 C3
Sandy La	41 D2
Seymour La	41 B2
Six Oaks Rd	41 C2
Spring Gdns	41 C2
Stragwyne Clo	41 B1
Street End	41 D2
Sycamore Clo	41 B1
Sylvan Dri	41 B3
Tanners Rd	41 C3
The Birches	41 C2
The Vineyard	41 C2
Thomas Rd	41 B2
Tornay Gro	41 B3
Tottenhale Clo	41 B3
Tutlands Rd	41 B2
Upper Crescent Rd	41 B2
Upper Toothill Rd	41 A5

Cracknore Rd	46 A2
Craven St	47 F2
Craven Walk	47 E2
Crosshouse Rd	47 G5
Cuckoo La	46 D5
Cumberland Pl	46 C1
Cumberland St	47 F3
Derby Rd	47 F2
Devonshire Rd	46 C1
Dorset St	47 E1
Duke St	47 F4
Durnford Rd	47 F1
East Gate St	46 D4
East Park Ter	47 E1
East St	46 D4
Elm St	47 G4
Elm Ter	47 G4
Elmfield	46 A2
Endle St	47 G4
Enterprise Way	47 F6
Evans St	47 E4
Exmoor Rd	47 F1
Exmouth St	47 E2
Floating Bridge Rd	47 G5
Forest View	46 D4
Four Posts Hill	46 B2
French St	46 D5
Gibbs Rd	46 D2
Gloucester Sq	46 D5
Golden Gro	47 F2
Graham Rd	47 E1
Graham St	47 H1
Granville St	47 G4
Grosvenor Sq	46 C1
Grove St	47 F4
Guildford St	47 G2
Guildhall St	46 D2
Hamtun St	46 D4
Handel Rd	46 C1
Handel Ter	46 C1
Hanover Bldgs	46 D3
Harbour Par	46 C3
Harrisons Cut	47 E3
Hartington Rd	47 F2
Havelock Rd	46 C2
Herbert Walker Av	46 A3
Hewitts Rd	46 A2
High St	46 D4
Hill La	46 B1
Holyrood Pl	46 D4
Houndwell Pl	47 E4
INDUSTRIAL ESTATES:	
Central Trading Est	47 G3
City Ind Park	46 B3
Itchen Bridge	47 G5
James St	47 F3
Jessie Ter	47 E5
John St	47 E5
Johnson St	47 F3
Josian Walk	47 F2
Kent St	47 G1
King St	47 E4
Kings Park Rd	47 E1
Kingsbridge La	46 C2
Kingsland Sq	47 F3
Kingsway	47 E2
Lansdowne Hill	46 D4
Latimer St	47 E5
Lime St	47 E4
London Rd	46 D1
Longcroft St	47 G3
Lower Canal Walk	47 E6
Madison St	46 D4
Manchester St	46 D3
Mandela Way	46 B1
Marine Parade	47 G4
Maritime Walk	47 F6
Maritime Way	47 E6
Market Pl	46 D5
Marsh La	47 F4
Melbourne St	47 F4
Millbank St	47 H1
Millbrook Rd	46 A1
Moorhead Ct	47 G6
Morris Rd	46 C1
Mountbatten Way	46 A2
Nelson Hill	46 B2
Neptune Way	47 F6
New Rd	46 D2
Newcombe Rd	46 C1
Nicholls Rd	47 F2
North Brook Rd	47 F1
North Front	47 E2
Northam Rd	47 F2
Northam St	47 E1
Northumberland Rd	47 F2
Ocean Way	47 F6
Ogle Rd	46 D3
Old Rd	47 F6
Orchard La	47 E5
Orchard Pl	47 E5
Oriental Ter	46 D5
Oxford Av	47 E1
Oxford St	47 E5
Paget St	47 G4
Palmerston Rd	47 E2
Park La	46 C1
Park Rd	46 A1
Park Walk	46 D2
Parsonage Rd	47 G1
Peel St	47 G2
Pirelli St	46 C3
Platform Rd	47 E6
Portland St	46 D3
Portland Ter	46 D2
Pound Tree Rd	46 D3
Princes Ct	47 G1
Princes St	47 G1
Queens Ter	47 E5
Queens Way	47 E5
Radcliffe Rd	47 G1
Regent St	46 D3
Richmond St	47 F5
Roberts Rd	46 A1
Rochester St	47 G2
Roman St	46 D4
Royal Crescent Rd	47 F5
Russell St	47 E4
Ryde Ter	47 G5
St Albans Rd	47 F1
St Andrews Rd	47 E1
St George St	47 E4
St Lawrence Rd	47 F5
St Mary St	47 F2
St Marys Bldgs	47 F3
St Marys Pl	47 E3
St Marys Rd	47 E1
St Matthews Clo	47 F2
St Michaels Sq	46 D5
St Michaels St	46 D5
St Peters St	47 F2
Salisbury Rd	46 D1
Saltmarsh Rd	47 F5
Sandhurst Rd	46 C1
Saxon Rd	46 A2
Scullards La	46 C3
Shirley Rd	46 A1
Simnel St	46 C4
Sir Georges Rd	46 A1
Solent Rd	46 B3
South Front	47 E3
Southbrook Rd	46 B2
Southern Rd	46 B3
Spa Rd	46 C3
Standford St	47 G4
Strand	47 E4
Sussex Rd	46 D3
Tasman Clo	47 F6
Terminus Ter	47 F5
The Polygon	46 C1
Three Field La	47 E5
Tintern Gro	46 B1
Town Quay	46 D5
Trafalgar Rd	47 E6
Trinity Rd	47 E2
Upper Bugle St	46 D4
Victoria St	47 G2
Vincents Walk	46 D3
Vyse La	46 D5
Water La	46 C1
Waterloo Rd	46 A1
Waterloo Ter	46 D1
Waverley Rd	46 A2
West Bay Rd	46 A3
West Marlands Rd	47 D2
West Park Rd	46 C2
West Quay Rd	46 B3
West Rd	47 E6
West St	46 D4
Western Esplanade	46 B2
Western Ter	47 F4
Westgate St	46 D5
William St	47 H1
Wilson St	47 G2
Windsor Ter	46 D2
Winkle St	46 D6
Winton St	47 E3
Wolverton Rd	47 F2
Wyndham Pl	46 B2
York Bldgs	46 D4
York Clo	47 H1
York Walk	46 D4

SOUTHSEA

A'Becket Ct	48 A2
Albany Rd	48 D3
Albert Gro	48 D3
Albert Rd	48 D3
Alec Rose La	48 B1
Anglesea Rd	48 B1
Ardwell St	48 D1
Armory La	48 A2
Ashburton Rd	48 B4
Ashby Pl	48 C4
Astley St	48 B2
Atherstone Walk	48 B2
Auckland Rd E	48 C5
Auckland Rd W	48 C5
Avenue de Caen	48 C5
Baileys Rd	48 D2
Beach Rd	48 D5
Beaufort St	48 D5
Bedford St	48 B2
Belle Vue Ter	48 B3
Belmont Pl	48 C3
Belmont St	48 C2
Berkshire Clo	48 D1
Blackfriars Clo	48 C1
Blackfriars Rd	48 C1
Blount St	48 B3
Bradford Rd	48 D2
Brandon Rd	48 D4
Bridgeside Clo	48 D1
Britain St	48 A1
Brittania Rd	48 B1
Brittania Rd N	48 B1
Brougham Rd	48 C2
Brunswick St	48 B2
Burgoyne Rd	48 D6
Burnaby Rd	48 A1
Bush St East	48 B3
Bush St West	48 B3
Caldecote Walk	48 B2
Cambridge Rd	48 A2
Campbell Rd	48 D3
Canal Walk	48 D1
Cannock Lawn	48 B3
Carlisle Rd	48 D1
Castle Clo	48 C3
Castle Rd	48 B3
Cavendish Rd	48 C3
Cecil Gro	48 B3
Cecil Pl	48 B3
Chadderton Gdns	48 A3
Chapel St	48 B3
Charles Dickens St	48 A1
Chatham Rd	48 A3
Chelsea Rd	48 D3
Chester Pl	48 C4
Chivers Clo	48 C2
Clarence Esplanade	48 A4
Clarence Par	48 B4
Clarence Rd	48 D5
Clarendon Rd	48 B4
Clifton Rd	48 B4
Clifton Ter	48 B4
Collingwood Rd	48 D4
Colpoy St	48 B2
Copper St	48 B3
Cottage Gro	48 C2
Cross St	48 C2
Cumberland Rd	48 D1
Dean St	48 A1
Denning Mews	48 C1
Diamond St	48 B3
Dorothy Dymond St	48 B1
Dugald Drummond St	48 C1
Duisburg Way	48 B4
Duncan Rd	48 D4
Dunsmore Clo	48 B2
Earlsdon St	48 B2
Eastern Villas Rd	48 D6
Eldon St	48 B2
Elm Gro	48 C3
Elm St	48 B3
Elphinstone Rd	48 B4
Exchange Rd	48 B1
Exmouth Rd	48 D4
Farthing La	48 A3
Flint St	48 B3
Florence Rd	48 D5
Fontwell Rd	48 C1
Fraser Rd	48 D2
Freestone Rd	48 C4
Friary Clo	48 C4
Froddington Rd	48 D1
Furness Rd	48 D6
Garden La	48 B3
Garden Ter	48 C4
Gloucester Mews	48 C2
Gloucester Pl	48 B3
Gloucester Ter	48 B3
Gloucester Vw	48 B3
Gold St	48 B3
Goodwood Rd	48 A3
Gordon Rd	48 D3
Grays Ct	48 A2
Great Southsea St	48 B3
Green Rd	48 C3
Greetham St	48 C1
Grosvenor St	48 C2
Grove Rd N	48 C3
Grove Rd S	48 C4
Guildhall Sq	48 B1
Guildhall Walk	48 B1
Halfpenny La	48 A3
Hambrook St	48 B3
Hamilton Rd	48 D4
Hampshire Ter	48 B2
Havelock Rd	48 D2
Hereford Rd	48 D3
High St	48 A3
Highbury St	48 A2
Hillborough Cres	48 D4
Holbrook Rd	48 D1
Hudson Rd	48 C2
Hyde Park Rd	48 C2
Hyde St	48 B2
Isambard Brunel Rd	48 C1
Jubilee Ter	48 B3
Kenilworth Rd	48 D5
Kent Rd	48 B3
Kent St	48 A1
King Henry I St	48 B1
King Richard I St	48 B1
King St	48 B2
Kings Rd	48 B2
Kings Ter	48 B3
Ladies Mile	48 C5
Landport St	48 B2
Landport Ter	48 B2
Lansdowne St	48 B2
Lennox Rd N	48 C4
Lennox Rd S	48 C5
Little Britain St	48 A1
Little Southsea St	48 B3
Livingstone Rd	48 D3
Long Curtain La	48 A4
Lord Montgomery Way	48 B1
Lowcay Rd	48 D4
Lower Forbury Rd	48 D2
Malvern Rd	48 D5
Maple Rd	48 C5
Margate Rd	48 B2
Marmion Av	48 D4
Marmion Rd	48 C4
Martells Ct	48 A2
Maxstoke Clo	48 D1
Meadow St	48 B2
Melbourne St	48 B1
Meriden Rd	48 B2
Merton Rd	48 C4
Middle St	48 B1
Montgomerie Rd	48 D2
Museum Rd	48 A2
Napier Rd	48 D4
Nelson Rd	48 C3
Netley Rd	48 C4
Netley Ter	48 C4
Nickel St	48 B3
Nightingale Rd	48 B4
Nobbs La	48 A2
Norfolk St	48 B2
Ockendon Clo	48 C2
Omega St	48 D1
Onslow Rd	48 D5
Ormsby Rd	48 B4
Osborne Rd	48 B4
Outram Rd	48 D3
Pains Rd	48 C2
Palmerston Rd	48 C4
Park Rd	48 A1
Park St	48 B2
Peacock La	48 A3
Pelham Rd	48 C3
Pembroke Clo	48 A3
Pembroke Rd	48 A3
Penny St	48 A3
Pier Rd	48 A4
Playfair Rd	48 D2
Plymouth St	48 C1
Port Royal St	48 D1
Portland Rd	48 C4
Portland St	48 A1
Poynings Pl	48 A3
Purbeck St	48 A1
Queens Cres	48 C4
Queens Gro	48 C4
Queens Pl	48 C3
Queens Way	48 C4
Quinton Clo	48 D1
Radnor St	48 C2
Raglan St	48 D1
Ravenswood Gdns	48 D5
Regent St	48 B3
Richmond Pl, Portsmouth	48 A1
Richmond Pl, Southsea	48 C4
Richmond Rd	48 D4
Rivers St	48 C1
Sackville St	48 B2
St Andrews Rd	48 D2
St Bartholomews Gdns	48 D3
St Catherine St	48 D5
St Davids Rd	48 D2
St Edwards Rd	48 B3
St Georges Rd	48 A1
St Georges Sq	48 A1
St Georges Way	48 A1
St Jamess Rd	48 C2
St Judes Clo	48 C4
St Michaels Rd	48 B1
St Nicholas St	48 A3
St Pauls Rd	48 B2
St Pauls Sq	48 B2
St Peters Gro	48 C3
St Simons Rd	48 D5
St Thomas's Ct	48 A2
St Thomas's St	48 A2
St Ursula Gro	48 D3
St Vincent Rd	48 D4
St Vincent St	48 B2
Sedgely Clo	48 C2
Serpentine Rd	48 B5
Serpentine Rd	48 C5
Shaftesbury Rd	48 B4
Silver St	48 B3
Slingsby Clo	48 B3
Somers Rd	48 D1
Somerset Rd	48 D5
South Normandy	48 A2
South Parade	48 D6
South St	48 B2
Southsea Ter	48 B3
Spring Gdns	48 B1
Stafford Rd	48 D3
Stanley La	48 C4
Stanley St	48 C4
Stanstead Rd	48 D2
Steel St	48 B3
Stone St	48 B3
Sun St	48 A1
Sussex Pl	48 B3
Sussex Rd	48 B3
Sussex Ter	48 C3
Sydenham Ter	48 D1
Taswell Rd	48 D5
The Circle	48 C4
The Mary Rose St	48 C1
The Queens Mall	48 C1
The Retreat	48 C3
The Thicket	48 C3
The Vale	48 C4
Tonbridge St	48 C4
Tyseley Rd	48 C1
Victoria Gro	48 D3
Victoria Rd Nth	48 D3
Victoria Rd Sth	48 D4
Villiers Rd	48 C5
Waltham St	48 B2
Warblington St	48 A2
Warwick Cres	48 C2
Waterloo St	48 C2
Wellington St	48 C1
Western Par	48 B4
White Swan Rd	48 B1
Wilberforce Rd	48 B3
Wilmcote Gdns	48 D1
Wilson Gro	48 D3
Wilton Pl	48 C4
Wilton Ter	48 C4
Wiltshire St	48 B2
Wimbledon Park Rd	48 D4
Windsor La	48 C2
Winston Churchill Av	48 B1
Woodpath	48 C3
Woodville Dri	48 A3
Worsley Rd	48 C3
Worthing Rd	48 D5
Wyndham Mews	48 A3
Yarborough Rd	48 C3
Yorke St	48 B2
Yves Mews	48 D4

TOTTON

Abbotts Field	49 A3
Alexander Clo	49 A3
Allerton Clo	49 A2
Amberley Ct	49 A5
Andrew Clo	49 A4
Arundel Rd	49 C3
Ashby Cres	49 A4
Ashby Rd	49 A4
Austen Clo	49 A5

Bagber Rd 49 B4
Bartley Rd 49 B5
Bartram Rd 49 C5
Beaumont Rd 49 C3
Belstone Rd 49 B4
Birchlands 49 A6
Bishops Clo 49 A3
Blackwater Dri 49 A2
Blackwater Mews 49 A2
Blenheim Clo 49 A5
Boniface Clo 49 A3
Brackley Way 49 A3
Briardene Ct 49 A3
Broadmeadow Clo 49 A4
Brockenford Av 49 C4
Brockenford La 49 C4
Bronte Clo 49 A5
Brookside 49 C6
Browning Clo 49 A6
Burnbank Gdns 49 B4
By-Pass Rd 49 C5
Calmore Rd 49 A3
Causeway Cres 49 A3
Chapel La 49 A6
Charnwood Clo 49 A2
Cheam Way 49 A2
Chiltern Clo 49 A6
Cocklydown La 49 A6
Commercial Rd 49 C3
Compton Rd 49 C3
Copse Clo 49 B5
Culford Av 49 B5
Culford Way 49 B5
Denbigh Clo 49 A6
Downs Park Av 49 C5
Downs Park Cres 49 C5
Downs Park Rd 49 D5
Drayton Pl 49 A4
Durley Cres 49 A6
Eddystone Rd 49 A1
Eling Hill 49 D6
Eling La 49 D5
Elldene Ct 49 A5
Ewell Way 49 A2
Eyre Clo 49 A5
Fairmead Way 49 A6
Fishers Rd 49 C5
Fox Hills 49 A6
Frampton Way 49 A6
Frampton Way 49 B5
Glen Rd 49 C4
Goldsmith Clo 49 A4
Graddidge Way 49 A4
Greenfields Av 49 B2
Greenfields Clo 49 B2
Hambert Way 49 B6
Hammonds Clo 49 B3
Hammonds Grn 49 A3
Hammonds La 49 B3
Hammonds Way 49 A3
Hamtun Cres 49 B2
Hamtun Gdns 49 B2
Harwood Clo 49 A3
Haselbury Rd 49 B4
Hawthorne Rd 49 A3
Hayward Clo 49 A4
Heather Clo 49 A4
Hemming Clo 49 B5
High St 49 D4
Highgrove Clo 49 A6
Hockleigh Dri 49 A6
Holly Hatch Rd 49 A5
Honeywood Clo 49 A2
Hounds Down Av 49 B6
Hounds Down Clo 49 B6
Hudson Ct 49 A5
Huntingdon Clo 49 B2
Hurst Clo 49 C3
Hymans Way 49 A4
Ibbotson Way 49 A6
INDUSTRIAL ESTATES:
Rushington Business
Park 49 B6
South Hampshire
Ind Park 49 A1
Itchin Clo 49 A1
Ivy Clo 49 A1
Jacobs Gutter La 49 B6
Jacobs Walk 49 B6
Jennings Rd 49 C3
Junction Rd 49 C4
Kayleigh Clo 49 A6
Kenmore Clo 49 A5
Kent Gdns 49 A5
Kilnyard Clo 49 A2
Kinross Rd 49 B4
Lackford Av 49 B5
Lawford Way 49 D5
Lexby Rd 49 D5
Library Rd 49 C3

Little Reynolds 49 A6
Long Beech Dri 49 A5
Longstock Cres 49 A4
Lydgate 49 A4
Lydlynch Rd 49 B4
Lynton Ct 49 A5
Main Rd 49 B6
Manor Clo 49 B5
Marchwood By-Pass 49 C5
Marybridge Clo 49 B5
Mayfield Av 49 B3
Maynards Rd 49 C4
Meacher Clo 49 A3
Meadow Clo 49 C6
Meredith Gdns 49 A5
Mill Rd 49 D4
Mill Way 49 A6
Milverton Clo 49 C5
Milverton Rd 49 C5
Monks Pl 49 A5
Montgomery Av 49 A3
Moons Cross Av 49 B6
Morpeth Av 49 C3
Mortimer Clo 49 A2
Mountbatten Rd 49 A3
Muppet Clo 49 B3
Myrtle Av 49 A5
Northlands Clo 49 A3
Northlands Rd 49 A3
Nutsey Av 49 A1
Nutsey La 49 A1
Nutwood Way 49 B1
Oak Mount Av 49 B3
Oakfield Rd 49 B4
Oaklands Av 49 B3
Oakleigh Cres 49 B5
Orchard Clo 49 B6
Osborne Rd 49 C4
Parkside 49 C6
Pembroke Clo 49 C3
Penhale Way 49 A5
Pentridge Way 49 A6
Pipers Clo 49 A5
Players Cres 49 B6
Popes La 49 C4
Portal Rd 49 A4
Powell Cres 49 C6
Reynoldsdale 49 A6
Ringwood Rd 49 A4
River View 49 C6
Roberts Rd 49 C5
Rose Rd 49 C6
Roseleigh Dri 49 A5
Rothbury Clo 49 A2
Rumbridge Gdns 49 C4
Rumbridge St 49 C5
Rushington Av 49 B5
Rushington La 49 A6
St Michaels Rd 49 B2
Salcombe Cres 49 A4
Salcombe Rd 49 A4
Salisbury Rd 49 A1
School Rd 49 C5
Selbourne Rd 49 A3
Serle Gdns 49 C4
Shakespeare Dri 49 A1
Shaw Clo 49 A4
Shelley Rd 49 A1
Sheridan Gdns 49 A5
Silkin Gdns 49 A5
Southern Gdns 49 B4
Spicers Hill 49 B6
Spicers Way 49 B5
Springfield Dri 49 B6
Stanley Rd 49 A2
Stannington Cres 49 C3
Stannington Way 49 C3
Station Rd North 49 D4
Station Rd South 49 D4
Stephenson Rd 49 A1
Stirling Clo 49 C2
Stirling Cres 49 C2
Sunny Way 49 C4
Sunset Av 49 B3
Sunset Rd 49 B3
Surrey Clo 49 A6
Sutton Rd 49 A2
Sylvia Cres 49 A2
Tedder Way 49 A4
Tennyson Rd 49 A1
Testbourne Av 49 A4
Testbourne Clo 49 A4
Testbourne Rd 49 A4
Testwood Av 49 B2
Testwood Cres 49 A1
Testwood La 49 B2
Testwood Pl 49 C3
The Bedfords 49 B2
The Drive 49 B5
The Retreat 49 C6

Thomas Clo 49 A5
Treeside Av 49 D4
Trevone Clo 49 A6
Trinity Ct 49 B1
Valley Rd 49 C6
Warwick Rd 49 B3
Water La 49 A3
Westfield Rd 49 B3
Westwood Ct 49 B1
Wilde Clo 49 A4
Windermere Gdns 49 B3
Windsor Rd 49 C4
Wingate Rd 49 A3
Yeomans Way 49 B3
York Clo 49 C3

WATERLOOVILLE

Albert Rd 50 B4
Aldermoor Rd 50 A6
Aldermoor Rd East 50 A6
Alexander Clo 50 A6
Allmara Dri 50 C6
Alsford Rd 50 A6
Alten Rd 50 A2
Andrew Cres 50 C5
Angelica Ct 50 D5
Angelo Cres 50 D3
Anmore Dri 50 A1
Anne Cres 50 C5
Aragon Ct 50 D3
Armstrong Clo 50 A1
Arnside Rd 50 B3
Aston Rd 50 B2
Avondale Rd 50 C3
Aysgarth Rd 50 B3
Badgers Brow 50 D5
Beaconsfield Av 50 C3
Beech Clo 50 C1
Beechwood Av 50 C5
Bell Cres 50 B5
Beresford Clo 50 B5
Bernina Av 50 A1
Bernina Clo 50 A1
Betula Clo 50 D6
Billet Av 50 C2
Bliss Clo 50 B6
Bluebell Clo 50 D5
Boxwood Clo 50 B5
Boyle Cres 50 B6
Bramley Clo 50 C3
Brightside 50 A5
Britten Way 50 B6
Broadlands Av 50 B4
Broadmeadows La 50 D4
Brookdale Clo 50 C3
Brooklyn Dri 50 C3
Broom Clo 50 D6
Bryony Way 50 D4
Buckland Clo 50 B1
Burlesdon Pl 50 A6
Burlesdon Rd 50 A6
Burnside 50 D2
Byrd Clo 50 C6
Campbell Cres 50 A6
Campion Clo 50 D5
Cavendish Clo 50 C3
Cavendish Dri 50 C3
Cedar Clo 50 B5
Chapel La 50 B4
Charles Clo 50 B5
Charlesworth Av 50 A1
Charlesworth Dri 50 A2
Charlesworth Gdns 50 A2
Charminster Clo 50 B3
Chaucer Clo 50 B1
Chilsdown Way 50 B6
Clinton Rd 50 A1
Clover Ct 50 D5
Coates Way 50 B6
Coltsfoot Dri 50 C6
Corbett Rd 50 A5
Covert Gro 50 D6
Cowan Rd 50 B6
Crofton Clo 50 A6
Crystal Way 50 D3
Cunningham Rd 50 B6
Curzon Rd 50 B6
Daisy Mead 50 D4
Danesbrook La 50 D4
Davidia Ct 50 D5
Days London Rd 50 A6
Deanswood Dri 50 B2
Deeping Gate 50 D4
Delft Gdns 50 B1
Delius Walk 50 B6
Dogwood Dell 50 C6
Dorcas Clo 50 D2

Dornmere La 50 D4
Dresden Dri 50 B1
Dryden Clo 50 B1
Durham Gdns 50 C6
Edwards Clo 50 C1
Elettra Av 50 A3
Elgar Walk 50 C6
Elizabeth Rd 50 B6
Elmwood Av 50 B5
Esher Gro 50 A1
Fabian Clo 50 D3
Fairborne Clo 50 B1
Fennel Clo 50 A2
Ferndale 50 D3
Firs Av 50 C1
Florentine Way 50 D4
Forest End 50 A4
Foxes Clo 50 B5
Frendstaple Rd 50 C6
Freshfield Gdns 50 B3
Gilbert Way 50 B6
Glamis Clo 50 D4
Gloucester Rd 50 C5
Gordon Rd 50 A5
Halifax Rise 50 C4
Hamble Rd 50 B6
Hambledon Rd 50 A2
Hampton Clo 50 D4
Hannah Gdns 50 C3
Hart Plain Av 50 B1
Hartwood Gdns 50 C1
Hasler Cres 50 A1
Hawkewood Av 50 A1
Heather Clo 50 C5
Hermitage Gdns 50 C3
High Trees 50 C5
Highfield Av 50 C2
Highfield Clo 50 C2
Holly Dri 50 D5
Holman Clo 50 D1
Holst Way 50 C6
Holyrood Clo 50 D4
Homer Clo 50 B1
Honeysuckle Ct 50 C6
Hopewood Mews 50 B4
Hopfield Clo 50 B4
Hulbert Rd 50 B3
Hunters Ride 50 B4
Hurstville Dri 50 C5
INDUSTRIAL ESTATES:
Pipers Wood Ind Pk 50 A3
Inhurst Av 50 D3
Ireland Way 50 B6
Jasmine Gro 50 D5
Jubilee Rd 50 B2
Kelly Rd 50 B5
Kentridge Rd 50 A6
Laburnum Rd 50 B5
Lambert Clo 50 B6
Lancaster Way 50 C5
Lantana Clo 50 C5
Laurence Av 50 C1
Laurus Clo 50 D6
Lavender Rd 50 D5
Lawnswood Clo 50 C1
Lobelia Ct 50 D5
Lombardy Rise 50 C6
London Rd 50 A6
Lower Bere Wood 50 C4
Lucerne Av 50 A1
Lugano Clo 50 A2
Lysander Way 50 D3
Mallow Clo 50 C5
Maralyn Av 50 B5
Margaret Clo 50 A2
Mark Ct 50 B3
Marlborough Clo 50 A6
Marlowe Ct 50 B2
Meadway 50 D2
Mey Clo 50 C5
Milk La 50 A5
Mill Rd 50 A5
Milton Par 50 B1
Milton Rd 50 B2
Mole Clo 50 C6
Montana Ct 50 D5
Montgomery Walk 50 A6
Mountbatten Dri 50 A5
Muriel Rd 50 B3
Newlands Rd 50 A6
Newlease Rd 50 C6
Norton Clo 50 B4
Novello Gdns 50 B5
Oak Clo 50 B1
Oakhurst Dri 50 D3
Oakmont Dri 50 C1
Oberon Clo 50 D3
Old Van Diemans Rd 50 A6
Osborne Rd 50 D4
Othello Dri 50 D3

Padnell Av 50 D1
Park La 50 D1
Philip Rd 50 C6
Pine Tree Gdns 50 D1
Place Cres 50 C6
Portland Rd 50 B4
Post Office Rd 50 A6
Primrose Clo 50 D4
Prince of Wales Clo 50 D4
Princes Dri 50 C6
Priory Gdns 50 B2
Purcell Clo 50 C6
Pyrford Clo 50 B1
Queens Gro 50 B6
Queens Rd 50 C2
Reedmace Clo 50 D4
Regency Gdns 50 B5
Relay Rd 50 A3
Riverdale Av 50 D4
Robinia Clo 50 D4
Rockville Dri 50 B4
Rosebay Ct 50 C6
Round Way 50 C3
Rowlands Av 50 B2
Royal Way 50 D4
Sage Clo 50 D6
St Georges Walk 50 B4
Salvia Clo 50 D5
Sebastian Clo 50 D3
Shaftesbury Av 50 A3
Silverdale Dri 50 A1
Silverthorne Way 50 A3
Silvester Rd 50 C1
Siskin Gro 50 D5
Sorrel Clo 50 D5
Springwood Av 50 C5
Spruce Av 50 D4
Spur Rd 50 B4
Stakes Hill Rd 50 A4
Staple Clo 50 A2
Stirling Av 50 C4
Stratfield Park 50 A3
Stratford Rd 50 D3
Sullivan Way 50 B6
Sunnymead Dri 50 A1
Sweet Briar Gdns 50 C5
Swiss Rd 50 B4
Sylvan View 50 C5
Tamar Down 50 D4
Tamarisk Clo 50 D6
Tansy Clo 50 D5
Tempest Av 50 D4
Tennyson Cres 50 B1
The Briar 50 A3
The Glade 50 D3
The Hassocks 50 D4
The Hundred 50 A2
The Link 50 D2
The Meadows 50 A3
Titus Gdns 50 D3
Treeside Way 50 C2
Trefoil Clo 50 D4
Upper Bere Wood 50 C4
Valentine Ct 50 D3
Venice Clo 50 D3
Vian Rd 50 B5
Victoria Rd 50 B6
Vine Coppice 50 B5
Wait End Rd 50 B5
Wallis Gdns 50 C2
Wallis Rd 50 B2
Walton Clo 50 B5
Warfield Av 50 B4
Warfield Cres 50 C4
Waterberry Dri 50 A2
Wellesley Clo 50 B4
Wellington Way 50 B4
Westside View 50 A2
Windrush Gdns 50 A4
Windsor Rd 50 A1
Winifred Rd 50 B3
Winscombe Av 50 D1
Woodlands Clo 50 B6
Woodsedge 50 D6

WHITCHURCH

Alliston Way 51 C4
Andover Rd 51 A5
Ardglen Rd 51 B3
Bell St 51 B3
Bell Yard 51 B3
Bellevue 51 B3
Bere Hill 51 C1
Bere Hill Clo 51 C2
Bicester Clo 51 B2
Blosswood Dri 51 A3
Blosswood La 51 A2